Horizon

JANUARY, 1959 • *VOLUME I, NUMBER 3*

HORIZON
A Magazine of the Arts

JANUARY, 1959 • VOLUME I, NUMBER 3

HORIZON is published every two months by
American Horizon, Inc., a subsidiary of American
Heritage Publishing Co., Inc., 551 Fifth Avenue,
New York 17, N. Y.
Single Copies: $3.95
Annual Subscriptions: $18.00 in the U.S. & Can.
$19.00 elsewhere

Second-Class postage paid at New York, N. Y.

HORIZON welcomes contributions but can assume
no responsibility for such unsolicited material.

COVER: The unknown lady on the cover sat for this luminous portrait in the middle of the fifteenth century. Her cone-shaped hennin is fastened with a velvet loop beneath her chin and pushed back to reveal the high, plucked forehead so much admired in her time. Aloof and tranquil, she gazes obliquely at her painter, the Flemish master Petrus Christus. The painting, *Portrait of a Young Girl,* is in the Gemäldegalerie, Museum Dahlem, Berlin. For an article on modern portrait painting, see page 95.

FRONTISPIECE: *The Goddess Music and Her Disciples* is a glowing example of the art of the Italian miniature painters who flourished at the Court of Anjou under the patronage of King Robert of Naples in the fourteenth century. The painting is a musical allegory illustrating the treatise *De Arithmetica, De Musica,* written by the fifth-century Roman philosopher Boethius. The musicians in this miniature are playing the favorite instruments of medieval Italy. In the center, the goddess of music plays the portative organ. Above her, in his golden circle, King David plucks the strings of his psaltery. Running clockwise are: the mandola, dancer with clappers, straight trumpets, kettle drums, bagpipe and shawm (or reed pipe), jingle drum, and vielle (or viol).

One of America's handsomest cities is also culturally
one of its most vivid. Here some of its symbols are
seen together from the top of Russian Hill, looking
out toward Telegraph Hill with its Coit Tower at
left. Below the height lies the North Beach section,
and beyond it is part of the great Bay Bridge that
connects the city with Oakland and Berkeley. In the
foreground, beside a cello symbolic of the city's
music, are works by San Francisco artists. From
left: a sculptured head by Stefan Novak; handwoven
textile by Lea Miller; a recent oil by Hassel Smith;
Figure with Flowers by David Park; an earlier
Smith, influenced by Clyfford Still; silver jewelry
by Bob Winston and ceramics by Antonio Prieto.

By ALLAN TEMKO

THE FLOWERING
OF
SAN FRANCISCO

Blessed by nature and individuality, the Bay Region

has become a magnet and proving ground of the arts

There is no city quite like it. San Francisco, compact and alive on its hills, commanding the vast landlocked harbor, is everywhere in motion, its irregular sky line broken by towers at every level of the terrain, the long streets rising straight to the crests of the hills and then dropping swiftly again, rows of jaunty frame houses clinging to slopes that branch downward suddenly to the shores of the Bay.

From Telegraph Hill, if the day is clear, the panorama extends for miles: blue water ringed with hills and peaks—Tamalpais directly north, Diablo off to the east—that are fresh green in spring after the winter rains, and then burn to a tawny brown beneath the summer sun. It is the Far West. No city is more "western" in its actual geography and history, and in its cherished myths.

But nowhere else in the West does a city such as this exist: proudly cosmopolitan, unmistakably urban, concentrated rather than diffused. Nowhere else in the United States, in fact, is there a city of comparable size, not to mention age, that provides facilities so rich and varied for civilized life. Not even Boston, which once could disdain the crude frontier town, now surpasses it as a home for the arts. New York alone is a more dynamic center of creativity; but New York is a world capital, and San Francisco is in the best sense a provincial seat, a small place, really, with a population of only about 800,000. Compared with New York's, its cultural resources may seem meager, but it is a measure of San Francisco that the comparison can be made at all.

The San Francisco Museum of Art, devoted to modern art exclusively, is as rich a collection as any outside of New

Nob Hill in the 1870's was a mixture of railroad barons' Italianate palaces and stark frame dwellings, most of which burned in the 1906 fire.

York. The same is true of the San Francisco Ballet, which in fact is the only resident company based outside New York. The Opera is one of three permanent grand opera companies in the United States, the others being in New York and Chicago; and not until the new Metropolitan is constructed in Manhattan, or until Louis Sullivan's Chicago Auditorium is refurbished, will there be a finer hall for music in this country than the San Francisco Opera House. The annual Art Festival, sponsored by the city, is the liveliest anywhere. If the weather holds, upwards of 300,000 people attend, and in a good year they purchase more than fifty thousand dollars' worth of art.

In some respects, of course, San Francisco is not in the class of the older metropolises of the eastern seaboard. Its Symphony, although a good orchestra, does not compare with the magnificent ensembles in New York, Boston, and Philadelphia. The De Young and the Legion of Honor are excellent provincial museums, but even if their historical collections were combined, they would be lost in the Metropolitan Museum of Art or the Art Institute of Chicago.

Yet what distinguishes San Francisco from a "second city" such as Chicago is precisely its frank refusal to compete with New York. Except perhaps during the Gilded Age, San Francisco has never suffered from a galling sense of provincial inferiority. Rather, it has been content to be

itself—and this reveals its degree of social poise. For the city would have little to gain and everything to lose if it attempted to become a Far Western Manhattan. As matters stand, it has much of the good that can usually be found only in larger cities—fine hotels, excellent jazz, serious bookstores—and it is relatively free of the bad. Blighted areas exist, as well as the Skid Row that Jack Kerouac, like William Saroyan before him, has described. Tourists scarcely realize that Chinatown, a festering legacy of the frontier, is one of the most congested slums in the world. But there is no overwhelming degradation of human life on the order of Harlem or the Chicago South Side.

Indeed, North Beach—a valley of white buildings between Russian and Telegraph hills—is the only authentic foreign quarter in the United States that is not an abject slum. On the contrary, it is a cheerful, sun-swept place, combining a Mediterranean ease of mood with first-generation American vigor and snap. Artists can live here, close to the School of Fine Arts on Chestnut Street, together with an even larger number of Bohemians who, as the critics of the so-called Beat Generation forget, are necessary to any community worth its salt. Rents are comparatively cheap, except in remodeled buildings or new apartment houses on the tops of the hills, which, like parts of Greenwich Village, have become fashionable. Furthermore, if San Francisco's famous restaurants are overrated (they are not nearly so good as the best in New York), the inexpensive *bistros* and cantinas of North Beach are not. And to have a good meal with wine for not much money is one test of a city.

San Francisco's founders were different from the plainer men and women who opened the Middle Border. California was a sea frontier, and its closest cultural associations were with New York, Boston, London, Paris, and Canton, rather than with Des Moines and St. Louis. The very cost of a voyage around the Horn prevented many men of humble condition from making the trip; and therefore a notable number of the pioneers came from middle-class and upper-class backgrounds. The taste of such men, in the arts as in *haute cuisine*, was equal to the best then prevailing in the East, and it set a standard for excellence.

The early city was nevertheless a rough boom town. There were few women. The mud in the streets was so deep that animals and drunken men drowned in it. Men carried side arms, and conditions were violent. Yet soon concert halls and theaters sprung up—more than a dozen of them—in a city that now possesses only two legitimate playhouses. Hunger for diversion, for relief from the sadness and loneliness of the frontier, was keen. Because of its remoteness, however, the city discovered that it would have to pay heavily if artists were to be induced to make the arduous journey west. San Francisco responded with a prodigality that became the talk of the civilized world. Fifty-dollar gold slugs were showered on the stage as applause broke out in the Metropolitan Theater and Maguire's Opera House.

Once, during a tumultuous ovation for Catherine Hayes, the Irish Linnet, a heavy slug struck the conductor on the ankle as he was escorting her from the stage.

The city could afford its extravagance. In the first two decades following the discovery at Sutter's Mill, some $800,000,000 in California gold and Nevada silver passed through the port. More important, so far as permanent wealth was concerned, was the fact that, while the mines were still producing, the Central Valley became one of the foremost wheat-producing areas in the world. Sawmills were going in the forests of redwood and Douglas fir. Commercial houses, shipping lines, and banks were established. Great fortunes were made, many of them permanent. A burgher patriciate began patronizing the fine arts. Descendants of early millionaires, bearing names such as Crocker and Zellerbach, remain wealthy today, and take a proprietary interest in the opera and art associations.

By the sixties San Francisco was a soundly constructed, law-abiding city of 100,000 inhabitants. In the pages of the *Overland Monthly*, *Golden Era*, and the *Californian*, the work of Mark Twain, Bret Harte, the articulate geologist Clarence King, and King's stubborn opponent, John Muir, began to appear. The University of California was founded in 1868, but it long remained hopelessly provincial, so that Josiah Royce would abandon Berkeley for Harvard because there was "no philosophy" on the Coast.

After the completion of the transcontinental railroad in 1869, San Francisco suffered the full onslaught of the Gilded Age. The incredible mansions of railroad millionaires disfigured Nob Hill, while the injustice of their land policies led Henry George to formulate the theory of the single tax and Frank Norris to write *The Octopus*. But railroad money endowed Stanford University in 1885; and in 1893 Mark Hopkins' family turned over the "castle" on Nob Hill to the Hopkins Institute of Art, which in time would become the California School of Fine Arts.

Slowly the foundations of a civilization were being laid, although taste in painting ran to Toby Rosenthal and William Keith, and in poetry to Ambrose Bierce's disciple George Sterling, who with a group of friends started a colony at Carmel on the coast early in this century. Then came the disaster of 1906; the city was never to be the same again.

It was to become better. After another generation passed, the arts—from the thirties onward—commenced to rise on a swell that has yet to reach its peak. The writings of John Steinbeck and William Saroyan were published. The tremendous bridges—heroic monuments of the age of the automobile—were flung across the Golden Gate and the Bay. Population doubled and redoubled until today it stands at 3,000,000 for the nine counties of the Bay Region. Almost as quickly as San Francisco itself became an important city of the nineteenth century, the Bay Area as a whole—a territory as large as Connecticut and Delaware combined—has become one of the great regional cities of the twentieth.

Today the city sponsors an annual art festival at which painters, sculptors, print makers, designers, and architects show their work.

Throughout the region, as well as in the city, are its artists. They are clustered about the universities and colleges, or gathered in the waterfront town of Sausalito, the fishing village of Inverness farther north on the coast, and, more isolated still, at Big Sur, where the spurs of the Santa Lucia Mountains sink into the Pacific on the most spectacular stretch of shore line in the United States. Very few of the artists are native westerners, although some came West as children. Most of them, like the bulk of the population, have arrived in the last twenty years from distant places: New York and Texas, Michigan, Iowa, and Missouri, and from Europe and Asia.

The suburbs are expanding in ever widening circles. The landscape has been seriously marred. Yet the Bay Region remains one of the most beautiful and pleasant places on earth, and the arts, rather than withering, are thriving where little fine art existed previously. The world has come to speak of Bay Region "styles" in architecture and painting, of Bay Region composers and writers; and rightly so, for if much of this art is not "regional" in a traditional sense, it nevertheless comes from an identifiable place. It is to preserve and enrich that identity, as a mark of civilization, that the new regional city of the Bay must strive as it doubles once again in population during the coming twenty-five years.

ARCHITECTURE *A strong, young school of design has been nourished but not confined by the native redwood tradition*

After the war it became apparent that the Bay Region was one of the few places in the United States and Europe where indigenous modern architecture existed. Beneath the eucalyptus trees on the Berkeley or Sausalito hills, looking out over the Bay, open on every side to the splendid outdoor environment, were redwood houses that were, as all fine regional architecture must be, inseparable from the landscape. Some of these homes, their shingles weathered to a deep golden brown, were half a century old. But going up beside them was the work of an able group of designers who shared the recognizable local tradition, yet were contemporary architects at the same time.

Significantly, the group had no isolated leading figure. Among the older men, near fifty or just past it in 1945, William Wurster had an international reputation among architects for his unaffected, carpenter-built houses of the thirties, and Gardner Dailey was known nationally; yet their work did not serve as a focusing influence on the generation coming up. Of the two, Wurster was the stronger. During the war, when other materials were scarce, he had a rare chance to use wood in a comparatively large building, the Schuckl cannery offices at Sunnyvale, whose handsome horizontals, emphasized by long vizors to keep off the sun, make it one of the best commercial structures in the country.

By far the greatest proportion of work in the region, however, was residential, and here redwood, the most common and inexpensive building material in California, served local designers wonderfully. The houses of Wurster and Dailey, of Mario Corbett, Fred Langhorst, Francis Joseph McCarthy, Josephy Esherick, and other men not yet forty (there were more than a dozen young designers of high competence) possessed a warm, informal ease and, at the same time, a profound dignity and refinement that in combination were altogether remarkable.

In conception the houses were reflections of a way of life that had long been developing in the West. Living areas extended directly out of doors, beneath shady, overhanging projections, to the decks and patios that Californians can use much of the year, and to gardens designed by landscape architects such as Thomas Church and Robert Royston. The houses were generally servantless—even wealthy women did their own cooking—and therefore the kitchens were often open to the rest of the house. Everywhere the houses were handsomely detailed: the natural texture of wood was enhanced by careful handling of proportion and line, which sometimes was virtually Japanesque, for the International School has no monopoly of clarity and simplicity in design. Nor did the flowing open plans appear to be abstract oblongs of space. The houses were strikingly personal, but they had none of the overpowering romanticism of Frank Lloyd Wright.

In fact, taken as a group working in a compact area, the Bay architects represented the main single force in this country that stood between Wright's Byronic *mystique* and the bare geometry of Internationalists such as Mies van der Rohe. For on the one hand they were unassuming in comparison with Wright; on the other they could see no reason why a single dogmatic formula, based on the cube and stripped to the structural bone, should be employed in a climate and terrain and an easy social milieu that bore no resemblance to the Germany of the 1920's. The Californians did not despise the machine. On the contrary, they took adroit advantage of modern technology and of industrial materials. They simply did not fall into the error of Le Corbusier of assuming that a machine aesthetic is in itself a guarantee of modernity.

This resistance to dogmatism has a strong local history. Today's designers have inherited the principles and, in some respects, the actual techniques of a magnificent earlier generation of Bay architects. Except for Bernard Maybeck,

HARRY REDL

Two young San Francisco architects, Myron Goldsmith and James Ferris, are seen with an experimental model of a bridge they have designed. Built of slender bands of prestressed concrete without steel reinforcement, the double span is intended to carry a four-lane highway over a deep rocky gorge of a width up to one thousand feet. A notable building (right) soon to be added to San Francisco's sky line is this tower for the American President Lines. It is the work of the Bay area architects Robert Anshen and Stephen Allen, seen here with their final model. Allen holds a sample of material to be used for the panels that form the facings on the street level of the structure.

Bernard Maybeck's Christian Science Church in Berkeley, built in 1912 with Oriental and Gothic motifs, is one of America's great churches.

who died in 1957 at the age of ninety-five, they remain almost unknown outside of the region: John Galen Howard, Willis Polk, Ernest Coxhead, Louis Christian Mullgardt, and, the only native Californian among them, Julia Morgan. They all used eclectic devices—Gothic tracery, Swiss balconies, Georgian doorways, Renaissance windows, Corinthian capitals. But in their freest work they fused historic elements into spontaneous expressions that belong to a high order of architecture in this country. Perhaps the masterpiece of the period, surpassed among American churches of its time only by Wright's Unity Temple, is Maybeck's Christian Science Church of 1912 in Berkeley, in which redwood is wedded with reinforced concrete piers, steel trusses, asbestos siding, and factory sash windows.

By their very beauty the finest creations of the Bay group call into question the concept of a carpenter tradition in an age when prefabricated shells, geodesic domes, and other revolutionary structures are showing the way toward a new, totally industrialized architecture. As labor costs mount and sites become more scarce and expensive, while population continues to grow, the custom-built house may become a prohibitive luxury. As it is, only a small fraction of the population can afford residences such as the Fred Ludekens house by Jack Hillmer, perhaps the most brilliant single

house erected in the region since the war, cantilevered outward above the rocky shore of the Bay.

In an ingenious attempt to provide well-designed homes at relatively low cost, the merchant builder Joseph Eichler has engaged a number of outstanding architects, not only local Regionalists, but Internationalists such as the sensitive Raphael Soriano; and with their plans he has mass-produced whole square miles of modern houses. Yet even good architecture cannot save the Eichler subdivisions from resembling other tracts in mood if not in appearance. ("One cross makes a church," a Bay architect quoted the Mexican proverb; "one hundred crosses make a cemetery.")

The crisis confronting the region, obviously, does not belong to the realm of architecture alone. More planning; more collective residential units, particularly public housing in blighted areas; more moderately tall buildings to replace petty business structures—are all needed. Redwood alone cannot cope with the problems involved. Its limitations were made clear when Ernest Kump, one of the area's excellent school architects, used the Regional style in a charming grammar school in San Jose, and then frankly turned to the International style in a large high school in the same city.

Historically, it is good to remember, the region has always relied on "international" styles in important buildings: the

One of the handsomest houses using California's indigenous redwood is this, designed by Jack Hillmer for the illustrator Fred Ludekens.

Victorian-Italianate style of the Montgomery Block of 1853; the early twentieth-century Beaux-Arts classicism of the San Francisco Civic Center; Willis Polk's *Art Nouveau* Hallidie Building of 1918, whose all-glass façade, an ancestor of Lever House on New York's Park Avenue, was the first in the United States.

Increasingly, however, as modern technology has grown more complex, the largest commissions in the region have gone to national rather than local firms. The nationwide organization of Skidmore, Owings, and Merrill, for example, has designed two of the city's new skyscrapers: the Crown Zellerbach Building whose façades of glass and aluminum, like so many of S.O.M.'s creations elsewhere in the country, have clearly been inspired by the work of Mies van der Rohe; and the more romantic Hancock Life Insurance Building, faced in polished granite and mounted on shaped concrete columns, which suggest the *pilotis* of Le Corbusier. When a tremendous hangar was required by United Airlines, the job was entrusted to the same firm's young design team of Myron Goldsmith and James Ferris, former assistants of Mies and Philip Johnson who had also studied under the great Italian Pier Luigi Nervi. The result was one of the most stirring pieces of structural design in the United States: cantilevered steel girders extending 142 feet in either direction from a central core of 40-foot high reinforced concrete columns of exceptional plastic beauty, the whole structure covering an area more than one hundred yards square.

This is the sort of overhang—rather than the projecting eaves of private houses—that will determine San Francisco's architectural future. The question remains, will the Bay architects simply yield the field to giant nationwide firms?

Perhaps the answer has already been provided by the American President Lines, a corporation with a long-standing historical stake in San Francisco. It has commissioned the local architects Robert Anshen and Stephen Allen, whose firm until a few years ago had an exclusively residential practice, to design a 21-story tower that will shortly go into construction. The skyscraper will receive a marked horizontal emphasis to reveal its cantilever construction; otherwise, its treatment will have a gusto that the pioneers would have relished. Its curtain walls will be of prefabricated concrete panels embedded with crushed white quartz; golden fins will project between the windows, partly for sun protection, partly to reduce the view to natural scale. Structurally the building will be International but its quality will be local and unique, which is one of the purposes of architecture.

THE FINE ARTS *Abstract painters and sculptors abound, though some have turned, amid lively controversy, to a new realism*

San Francisco held its first exhibition of modern art at the Panama-Pacific Exposition of 1915. The crowds were friendly and curious. By far the most impressive exhibits came from France: impressionists and post-impressionists, four oils by Picasso, and fifteen prints by Matisse. Of the Californians shown, there was no one whose name is remembered today except by antiquarians.

Twenty years later the situation had not changed. When the San Francisco Museum of Art was installed at the Civic Center in 1935, the inaugural show was dominated by French painters. The next year Dr. Grace Morley, a student of French civilization, was appointed to the directorship, a post she was to hold with distinction until a few months ago. Under her regime the museum flourished, and although its emphasis remained on the contemporary Europeans, its policy was "to stay close to the growing edge" of modern art, and to show local painters also. How close San Francisco was to the borders of a whole new phase of the contemporary movement, no one quite realized when the museum accorded a one-man show in 1943 to the painter Clyfford Still.

Until he came to San Francisco in 1941, Still had painted in isolation in the Northwest. An outspoken rebel, he had reflected on the course of European painting since the Renaissance and decided that, down the centuries through cubism, it was pretty much worthless as far as he was concerned. As he saw it, it had begun by confining space within mechanical perspective, and it was ending by cutting up space and rearranging it in an artificial puzzle. In the eyes of this solitary westerner, painting should be nothing less than the absolute liberation of space—space as he knew it in the vast unfenced country that was so true and savage it needed no housekeeping—moving in planes of light and color in a totality that could not be rationally analyzed but that had to be felt.

At first he attempted to convey this idea in expressionist landscapes. Then, about the time he came to the Bay Region, he adopted a new style, totally abstract, utterly

One of San Francisco's leading sponsors of contemporary art is Dr. Grace McCann Morley, the recently retired director of the Museum of Art. On the facing page she is surrounded by some of the works the museum acquired during her tenure. From left: Kandinsky's Brownish; *Matisse's* Sarah Stein *and* Girl with Green Eyes; *and the sculpture* Presence *by the late San Francisco artist Adaline Kent. At right is Hassel Smith, one of the Bay Region's leading abstractionists, in his studio before some of his canvases.*

different from the attempts of the anarchic New Yorker Jackson Pollock, or the atomizing calligrapher Mark Tobey in Seattle, to break away from tradition. Still's paintings were heavily, almost brutally, brushed and thickened deeply with the knife. The colors were somber: browns, blacks, morose reds. Narrow vertical openings, in sardonic yellow or white, twisted downward through jagged planes, like lightning flashes that illuminated the distances receding in darkness to every side.

Still's influence erupted powerfully at the end of the war, when an extraordinary set of young teachers and students, many just out of the service, assembled with him at the California School of Fine Arts. The head of the school, Douglas MacAgy, encouraged every kind of experiment.

In the meantime a number of San Franciscans developed their own abstract-expressionist styles: Edward Corbett, Richard Diebenkorn, Hassel Smith, David Park, Elmer Bischoff, Robert McChesney, Frank Lobdell, Walter Kuhlman, Ernest Briggs. Others—John Hultberg was one—never abandoned recognizable images but turned toward a semi-surrealism. What distinguished them as a group was their diversity, not their uniformity.

Then in 1950, as suddenly as it had flowered, the school declined. MacAgy quit his directorship in order to become a film maker, and was replaced by the more conservative Ernest Mundt. Many of the avant-garde young painters left the region, partly to seek stimulation elsewhere. Still moved on to New York, where he remains today, aloof and increasingly mystical. Sam Francis went all the way to Paris, where his huge oils have been acclaimed as the product of *"L'Ecole du Pacifique."*

In many cases the change of scene was beneficial. Diebenkorn, for instance, left for the University of New Mexico; there the colors of the Southwest—sun-driven oranges and yellows and the harsh rose tones of the desert—appeared in

ROBERT MC CHESNEY

13

canvases which were governed by bars of blue or purple like the dramatic landscape itself.

Gradually some of the Bay painters returned and found that a new local force had emerged. Or rather, an old one had changed direction and found new vigor. Its center, if any place, was the University of California, to which David Park had moved from the School of Fine Arts.

Park in 1950 abruptly abandoned abstract expressionism and turned frankly to representational painting. He was the first noteworthy artist in the country to make the break. In 1954 Park's friend Bischoff also went over to representationalism. Three years later, in the most significant defection yet made from abstract expressionism, Diebenkorn joined them. After a period of uncertainty, he appears to have found himself. He now paints human figures and landscapes that move with a forthright energy and coherence entirely his own. They are marked by brilliant foreground displays of color—for example, a Delacroix-style divan, boldly striped with red and gold—and then move in vigorous strokes to complex and remote blues and violets.

Although the early revolutionary impetus of abstract expressionism has subsided, the region remains a stronghold of the movement. New artists with explicit statements of their own, such as Julius Wasserstein and Jay de Feo, have appeared. The work of older painters remains impressive. Hassel Smith continues to be the most spirited and unpredictable of them: his wild calligraphy spurts ambiguously into clouds of bright yellow or blue. The work of perhaps half a dozen other artists, from the fastidious golden and black compositions of McChesney and the solid conceptions of Lobdell, Kuhlman, and Budd Dixon to the diffused,

almost chaotic energy of James Kelly, displays a range of talent that would honor any city.

In sculpture, too, the region stands divided between abstract and representational camps. Robert Howard's ingenious moving objects are sometimes recognizable as dinosaurs and birds, but where he has depended on pure abstraction to draw the strength of wood from the living grain, his work has seemed most rich and original. His late wife, Adaline Kent, was a consistent abstractionist whose carefully worked out static forms, although relatively small in scale, occasionally achieved monumental force. Miriam Hoffman's mythic heads—some as gigantic, in reinforced concrete, as unearthed Incan idols—have a strange mystical grandeur that does not depend on their figurative elements at all. Stefan Novak is a younger sculptor who has stayed close to recognizable images, but in his recent vigorous bronzes—heads, candelabras, female forms—has developed a style that is now nearly abstract.

Whatever their personal idiom, all of these sculptors work in terms of the classic concept of solid objects. Even when the objects are pierced by apertures (as in the case of Adaline Kent's *Presence*, shown on page 12) their solidity is emphasized. But there is a newer sculpture that scarcely deals in solids at all, but rather in open constructions of wire, tubing, and other flexible materials, in which sheer space forms an integral part of the whole design. This school is represented in San Francisco by Claire Falkenstein (whose *Sun, No. 14* is also illustrated below). Last year she returned from work in Paris and Rome with a technique of using brazed wire and copper tubing, lacing them with melted glass and gold and silver in floating oval webs that she calls "Suns."

Even in the crafts the division between abstract and nonabstract thinking runs deep. The Bay Region now has literally hundreds of craftsmen: there are thirty-eight societies of weavers alone. At their best they are first-rank artists of national stature—potters such as Antonio Prieto and J. B. Blunk; Bob Winston and other jewelers; tapestry maker Mark Adams and weavers such as Lea Miller and Trude Guermonprez.

A coming generation of painters and sculptors, fully as talented as the preceding one, has commenced to emerge. The schisms that have divided the Bay Region's artists during the past decade have only revealed the vitality of a creative milieu which, outside of New York, easily surpasses any other in the United States.

FRED LYON

Long known as an abstractionist, Richard Diebenkorn recently made news by turning to a way of art disdained by many of his colleagues —the representation of natural objects and human forms. On the facing page he is seen standing in his Berkeley studio. Left, Claire Falkenstein, a prominent San Francisco sculptor, displays one of her open constructions of wire and tubing. It bears the title Sun, No. 14.

LITERATURE

> *The coast hills at Sovranes Creek:*
> *No trees, but dark scent pasture drawn thin*
> *Over rock shaped like flame;*
> *The old ocean at the land's foot, the vast*
> *Gray extension beyond the long white violence;*
> *A herd of cows and the bull*
> *Far distant, hardly apparent up the dark slope;*
> *And the gray air haunted with hawks:*
> *This place is the noblest thing I have ever seen.*
>   *No imaginable*
> *Human presence here could do anything*
> *But dilute the lonely self-watchful passion.*

The style of these lines, like the coastline which inspired them, is unmistakable. In the twentieth century, the poet Robinson Jeffers alone commands this grand manner: Miltonic, in proximity with God or with the deity Nature; personalized by the flying hawks; enriched by mythological beasts; anchored on rock, constructed of rock, like Jeffers' own Tor House and tower at sea-pounded Carmel Point. And whatever else the poem may be, it is Californian. If the sentiment risks banality and frequently succumbs to it in Jeffers' poorer poems, the risk is worth all the failures for the moments of success. No younger poet would attempt the eloquence of "This place is the noblest thing I have ever seen"; much less bring it off. But the context saves the line, and the context is nothing less than the land and the ocean and the gray air.

Northward, across the Santa Cruz Mountains, is Jeffers' most articulate critic, the academician Yvor Winters of Stanford, himself a poet, and on occasion a fine one. In the name of classical humanism he calls Jeffers' romanticism to account, finding its rhetoric lax and unclear (although perhaps not in the lines quoted) and its mystical ideology suicidal. Winters' quarrel with Jeffers, when all is said, is merely a skirmish in a great battle in modern thought that has been waged between the romanticist, the Promethean hero who grapples with Nature but is essentially one with Nature, and the classicist who would impose rational order on Nature and live according to rules. What gives the quarrel significance is that it is being fought by doughty opponents in California, a place that was a wilderness when Rousseau contended with Voltaire. In one guise or another, representatives of both camps can be found there today.

The rocky coastline at Big Sur, south of Monterey and Carmel, forms a background for two novelists: Dennis Murphy, who lives close to the winding road in left center, and Henry Miller, whose home is on a ridge in the hills.

HARRY REDL

Poets abound in the Bay Region. Here several foregather in the garden of a North Beach restaurant called the Spaghetti Factory. From left, first row: Rosalie Moore who, with Jean McGahey (next to her), belongs to a group called Activists ("every word is active"); James Broughton, also a playwright and moviemaker; Madeline Gleason; Robert Horan and Don Geiger, who both teach at the University of California. In center, behind them, is Ruth Witt-Diamant, a leading figure in the West Coast literary world, who conducts the Poetry Center at San Francisco State College at which all these poets have read. Back row, from left: Harold Witt, lyricist; Brother Antoninus, O. P., a Dominican lay brother; Vincent McHugh, also known as a folk historian and novelist; Robert Beloof; James Scheville, a poetic dramatist.

At Big Sur on the same spectacular southern coast, the onetime expatriate novelist Henry Miller, for example, lives in Rousseauistic withdrawal from the American Dream which he has called "The Air-Conditioned Nightmare" ("The newspapers lie, the radios lie, but the streets howl with truth"). His simple house stands 1,000 feet above the twisting highway which reminds him of the French Riviera's Grand Corniche; the view to sea extends for miles. Isolated, but not quite, for although Big Sur has been discovered by well-heeled gentry and is being invaded by suburban comforts (even Miller, who once climbed to Partington Ridge with his groceries in tow in a little wagon, now has an old Cadillac), it remains one of the country's most genuine artists' colonies. A few minutes away by car—twelve miles by foot—Miller has a neighbor such as Dennis Murphy, whose novel *The Sergeant* was perhaps the most skillfully constructed book by an American under thirty last year.

Two hundred miles north, at the opposite end of the region, Jessamyn West lives in the golden Napa wine country. Here she composes her private visions of Americana, which for all their fastidious craftsmanship, occasional folk whimsy, and hushed Quaker calm are not so politely written as they may at first appear. Like John Steinbeck, she has entered the long valleys of California and noticed thwarted ambitions in queer rural towns ("Tom Wolfe's My Name"). At Napa she tends her horses, and, much as Edith Wharton read the Lost Generation, she reads Jack Kerouac.

Between Napa and Big Sur the region is filled with writers. Some have established reputations or, like the writer of sea stories Calvin Kentfield in Sausalito and the Berkeley novelist George P. Elliot, are just beginning to make them. Some are unknown except in little magazines. A few, such as Erskine Caldwell in San Francisco and C. S. Forester in the Berkeley Hills, are famous; they live in the region because they find it pleasant—more pleasant, say, than New York or Hollywood—but never write about it, as they might not write of Majorca if they chose to live there.

Most writers, of course, have not had the success of Caldwell or Forester, and a surprisingly large number of them support themselves in the groves of academe. The region's universities and colleges have become massive patrons of letters. The faculties of the University of California, Stanford, San Francisco State College, and even smaller schools such as St. Mary's include whole strings of writers and poets, recruited as deliberately as halfbacks, or rather coaches, because programs in creative writing are under way on all the campuses. Thus far they have produced competence rather than brilliance, which is the mark of the instructors themselves: Wallace Stegner at Stanford, Mark Schorer at Berkeley.

Walter Van Tilburg Clark is probably the only one of the teacher-novelists who can rest assured of a place in our literature. He publishes little, but *The Track of the Cat* and *The Ox-Bow Incident* are profound moral fables of the West. San Francisco State College, where he teaches, is a lively place that has been overshadowed by Berkeley and Stanford and deserves more notice than it receives. Among the younger men on the faculty is Mark Harris, whose slight early work (*Bang the Drum Slowly*, *The Southpaw*), couched in a curiously pretentious baseball idiom, gave no indication that his recent *Something About a Soldier* would be one of the best comic novels yet written about the last war.

The college also supports a unique Poetry Center, directed by Ruth Witt-Diamant, Dylan Thomas' friend, and for that matter the friend of every poet. She is one of San Francisco's great personages. Virtually every poet of stature in the United States, as well as all the good local poets, have given public readings at the center. Here is a meeting ground for the academic world and the world at large; and when they meet, they often clash with beneficial results. The nonteaching poets, as can be expected, have little love for the august milieu of the large universities. Not only do they reject the contrived and wooden books of professor-authors such as George R. Stewart (*Fire*, *Storm*) and Eugene Burdick (*The Ninth Wave*, *The Ugly American*), but they have outright contempt for the even larger number of professor-critics who, like the "old, learned, respectable bald heads" in William Butler Yeats's satirical poem "The Scholars," "edit and annotate" the passionate lines of young men. With this sort of genteel academic criticism in mind, Jack Spicer wrote in "Berkeley in Time of Plague":

> *Plague took us and the chairs from under us,*
> *Stepped cautiously while entering the room*
> *(We were discussing Yeats); it paused a while*
> *Then smiled and made us die.*
>
> *Plague took us, laughed and reproportioned us,*
> *Swelled us to dizzy, unaccustomed size.*
> *We died prodigiously; it hurt a while*
> *But left a certain quiet in our eyes.**

*©1957 BY GROVE PRESS, INC.

Beyond showing the discipline and the anger of a member of a generation that has been described as "beat" or passive, the poem reveals that styles other than the ungoverned expressionism of Allen Ginsberg exist in the region. They were in fact fully developed before Ginsberg's arrival in 1955 and his subsequent publication of the famous insurgent poem "Howl"—overwritten and often melodramatic, yet one of the most furious indictments of American civilization made in our time. (Ginsberg and Kerouac, it should be noted, are essentially easterners, with their main artistic stake in New York; shortly before they attracted national attention they headed back, and do not live in the region today.) In technique Spicer's poem can stand very well beside the work of, say, Josephine Miles, who after Robert Horan is the finest poet teaching at the university. She, too, is aware of a non-academic world outside the classroom:

> *. . . there the whole trash*
> *Flats of Berkeley floated in suspense*
> *Gold to the Gate and bellied to the redwood Cottages.*

There are no generalities to be made about the region's poets and authors, which is a sign of their strength. Their themes often may be localized—they can make witty jokes, as Lawrence Ferlinghetti does, about Coit Tower—but at their best their meaning is universal. In Ferlinghetti's North Beach bookstore, City Lights, are the stacked outpourings of perhaps fifty little-known poets and writers. Ferlinghetti not only sells but publishes their work (and, incidentally, stood trial for publishing Allen Ginsberg's "Howl," charged with selling obscene literature, and was acquitted.)

HARRY REDL

Robinson Jeffers

Poets, as W. H. Auden predicted in the thirties for the years after the war, are "exploding like bombs." If some of the bombs are duds, it makes little difference. Work is going on. It is uneven in quality, but often surprisingly good; certainly it compares with the overall work of poets the same age anywhere else in the world. Few poets anywhere, old or young, coming to ask the riddle that has always been the business of poets, can see the Sphinx with the clear beauty of Robert Horan:

> *The Sphinx, a singular medallion,*
> *a tomb at evening, a field where nothing is watered,*
> *and nothing in time is altered*
> *but the imperceptible erasures of the wind.*
> *A perfect meditation, requiring no nourishment*
> *other than itself. A fact, like a rose.*

THE PERFORMING ARTS

Still provincial in spirit, the region is fostering first-rate talents in music, theater, and dance

The more piano, Ralph Waldo Emerson remarked when instruments were first shipped to the West, the less wolf. Optimistic as he was, Emerson could not foresee that within a century California would become a center of musical composition as advanced as any in the world. Until his death in 1951 Los Angeles was honored by the presence of Arnold Schönberg, and Igor Stravinsky lives there still. To the Bay Region came other distinguished foreigners—Darius Milhaud to Mills College in Oakland and Ernest Bloch to the University at Berkeley. The American Roger Sessions also joined the university's faculty; and after the late war an extraordinarily gifted group of young men assembled in the region to study and teach in the graduate school of composition that he directed. Their impact on contemporary music, now that their mature work has begun to be played, promises to be enormous.

Of the new generation Leon Kirchner, who will be forty this month and teaches with Milhaud at Mills, is thought by many to be the nation's most powerful young composer. His work explodes with personal force like a Joycean expression of self, drawing upon time past, flowing broadly through time present, possessing a multidimensional wealth of conception that is rare in contemporary music. Kirchner himself has best described his work in score markings that range from "Wild!" and "Appassionato!" to "hesitantly" and "reflective." Yet at its furthest intensity—when the composer in the Trio for Violin, 'Cello, and Piano asks that a passage come "from nowhere . . . almost out of control" —the music is never really out of control but part of an integrated vision of the modern world. In his Sinfonia of 1951 and especially the Piano Concerto of 1953, which the composer himself has recorded with stunning strength with the New York Philharmonic under Dimitri Mitropoulos, Kirchner showed that he could express such a vision on a symphonic scale rivaling that of the great nineteenth-century composers. In shorter works such as the Sonata Concertante and Second String Quartet he also revealed decisiveness of purpose that showed him finally to be free of obligation to his early masters, Bartók, Schönberg, and Sessions. Now he is composing an opera in which all the elements of his work can be brought into play: tremendous scale, pure lyricism, dense orchestration, and a central philosophical theme.

Two years younger than Kirchner is Andrew Imbrie, who teaches at Berkeley and whose Violin Concerto was given its *première* by Robert Gross and the San Francisco Symphony at the festival which inaugurated the university's new music buildings last spring. Turbulent but astringent, and given a certain martial quality by sudden calls on the drums, the concerto was a striving and emphatic piece of music. With his Second String Quartet it was the best work to date of a fine composer who, like Kirchner, is now writing an opera. Another high moment of the festival was Seymour Shifrin's Serenade for Five Instruments, a lucid and accomplished work that revealed a personal style of strong melodic beauty. Shifrin, too, is a professor at the university and has been commissioned to do an orchestral work for the Minneapolis orchestra.

The festival was only one example of the substantial material encouragement given to serious music by the university, as well as by Mills College and other institutions in the region. Yet it also revealed some of the handicaps that face the excellent local composers, of whom there are perhaps a dozen others of serious caliber, including Jerome Rosen and William Denny. For in a region that maintains a symphony orchestra and that produced Isaac Stern, Leon

HARRY REDL

Known for their nationwide and foreign tours, the members of the Griller Quartet (named after Sidney Griller, far left on the facing page) practice in a garden of a Berkeley home. They are musicians in residence at the University of California. Right, Leon Kirchner is both an outstanding young composer and a pianist noted for his interpretation of Mozart as well as of modern music. Like Darius Milhaud, he teaches composition at Mills College.

Fleisher, and Yehudi Menuhin, it is difficult today to hear contemporary music properly performed. There are no resident instrumentalists of the first international rank, with the exception of the older pianist Egon Petri, who teaches at the San Francisco Conservatory, and Kirchner himself, who is a pianist and an able conductor as well as a composer.

As for the San Francisco Symphony, it is a delicate subject at present. Imbrie's Concerto fared ill—as unfamiliar music frequently does—in the hands of the new conductor, Enrique Jorda. In a community that had grown accustomed to a conductor of Pierre Monteux' stature and dash, it seems a pity that a man of equal gifts did not succeed him.

If the Symphony under Jorda has failed to play as much new music as it should, the same cannot be said of the Little Symphony directed by Gregory Millar, a thirty-five-year-old Canadian who is also conductor of the Monterey Symphony. The Little Symphony is ambitious, fresh, and vigorously conducted. It suffers from lack of rehearsal time —a euphemism for lack of financial support—but it nevertheless provides San Francisco with one of the country's few chamber orchestras.

In fairness to the Bay Region one must resist the continual temptation to compare it with New York and Los Angeles, where topnotch musicians can support themselves in the motion picture and television studios rather than by teaching and occasional concerts. San Francisco, not altogether unfortunately, is considered a small town by the communications industry; and, of course, that is what it is.

Provincialism has two sides, as Josiah Royce realized even after the crudity of early California compelled him to make a career as a philosopher in genteel New England. "The better aspect of our provincial consciousness is always the longing for the improvement of the community," he wrote in 1902. Although a Milhaud, a Sessions, coming from the older societies of Europe and the East Coast, can act as musical catalysts, and although an artist such as Kirchner can be formed in the community and remain as a stimulus, it is the responsibility of the region as a whole to coalesce into a civilized entity. This is precisely what the Bay Region is gradually accomplishing with the means at its disposal.

The university, for example, has had the wisdom to establish the Griller Quartet as musicians in residence. They are not a great quartet, as the Budapest undeniably is a great quartet. At times they are not even a really good one, as when they attempt to cope with Imbrie's music. But they are a splendid *regional* quartet—which is what matters. They easily surpass any quartet that existed previously in the region on a year-round basis. And they are, of course, teachers as well as musicians. Perhaps a quartet will arise from among their students that will in turn surpass them.

For art continues to develop where it must, among the young. Although San Francisco endures the disgrace of its two outmoded and shabby theaters and of first-run plays presented only by traveling companies from the East, the

Ann Halprin (right, foreground), organizer of a modern dance group in San Francisco, is here seen teaching in an outdoor theater designed by her husband, Lawrence Halprin, a well-known landscape architect.

little theater movement is thriving. In San Francisco there are the Interplayers, the Opera Ring, and the Playhouse; in Berkeley there is the charming Company of the Golden Hind; there are others at Palo Alto, Tiburon, and Alameda. Of them all, the Actor's Workshop, which represented the United States at the Brussels Fair last fall with its performance of *Waiting for Godot*, is by far the most impressive. In fact, it is as audacious as one could wish a repertory company to be. The directors, Jules Irving and Herbert Blau, have attempted everything from Greek tragedy and Restoration comedy to Chekhov and Giraudoux. They have repeatedly staged the work of the region's playwrights, of whom Blau himself is the most outstanding. Blau is also a talented director. If his *Godot* and *Iceman Cometh* were too explicit, too literal, the plays nevertheless were treated with an interpretative vigor that one does not expect to find in a "little" theater.

And there is the dance—not only the classical ballet that has also been representing the nation abroad, in Asia and South America, but also modern dancers such as Ann Halprin. Her school in Marin County lies out-of-doors in the midst of madroña and eucalyptus. Its open-air theater was designed by her husband, landscape architect Lawrence Halprin. Nearby is their redwood house designed by William Wurster and his partners Theodore Bernardi and Donn Emmons.

Half a century ago Josiah Royce, the philosopher who had deserted California for Harvard, had hoped for just this sort of living evidence of a civilization. "Let the province more and more seek its own adornment," he urged. "Local pride ought above all to center . . . about the determination to give the surroundings of the community nobility, dignity, beauty. We Americans spend far too much of our early strength and time upon injuring our landscapes, and far too little upon endeavoring to beautify our towns and cities. We have begun to change all that, and . . . I can strongly insist that no community can think of any creation of genuine beauty and dignity . . . too good for its own deserts."

The change which Royce optimistically noted is gaining momentum. The Bay Region's artists have shown that a level of civilization of which he could only dream is possible today in the Far West. It is now up to the region to accept their art as an inseparable element of daily life, to honor the old philosopher as a prophet, and to make his vision a reality more splendid than he would have dared to predict.

Allan Temko teaches at the University of California in Berkeley and is writing a cultural history of the state. He is the author of Notre-Dame of Paris, *a biography of the cathedral.*

THE NEW YORK *Tribune*,
FOUNDED 1841 BY HORACE GREELEY

ACQUIRED 1871 BY WHITELAW REID

COMBINED WITH THE NEW YORK
Herald 1924 BY OGDEN REID

CONTROLLING INTEREST ACQUIRED
1958 BY JOHN HAY WHITNEY,
UNITED STATES AMBASSADOR
TO THE COURT OF ST. JAMES

A MEMORANDUM

From: Horace Greeley

To: John Hay Whitney

Subject: How to Compete with
          The New York Times

Young man, I'm glad to see it's you that has come into possession of the legacy I left. Now there's poetic justice, to find a grandson of my old friend John Hay back at the *Tribune*. You know, I always thought your grandfather would have made a corking good newspaperman, if he hadn't been so tempted by the wiles of diplomacy. The same goes for my friend Reid: Whitelaw would have done a far sight better to mind our paper than go gallivanting about in knee breeches as ambassador to the Court of St. James. I hear you have been doing some of the same yourself, though they don't put you in knee breeches any more. I won't hold it against you, my boy, just so long as you peel off your coat and do right by our *Tribune*. Welcome back! I greet you at the start of a career that may advance our profession, our party, and our Republic. I'm told all three could stand a lift.

But why, for tarnation's sake, when you bought up my *Tribune* did you have to go and buy the *Herald* part of it, too? That old Democratic rapscallion James Gordon Bennett built up his *Herald* just to spite me, and I turned in my

grave when the Reids bought out his rag. In my day, I never bought—I fought. What a day of giant battles it was, trading blows with Bennett, with Dana of the *Sun*, with Bryant of the *Post*! Where are they all now? All you have to contend with is that latecomer, the New York *Times*. How journalism has shrunk! I wrestled with mighty men; you seem to face an encyclopedia.

They tell me you have ample money to throw in against the *Times*. Where did you get it all from, son? Not from grandfather Hay, I should think: the most I remember paying him on the staff was $65 a week. I suppose your people on the Whitney side did pretty well with their investments in street railways—even though there's hardly a streetcar left around. But don't let all this money be a handicap to you. Money wasn't what I used to build the *Tribune*. Ten years after I started it with just $1,000, a fellow whom I had trained in my own office broke away and raised $100,000 to start the *Times*; but did that make his paper a hundred times better than mine? What did Editor Henry Raymond announce as his policy when he started the *Times*

By WILLIAM HARLAN HALE

with all that cash? "There are very few things in the world which it is worth while to get angry about," he said, with a superior air. Pah! Aren't there, though! So long as I was around, the *Tribune* for its part *did* get angry—often. It also got enthusiastic. It peppered the opposition, it ran out rascals, it cried hosanna and waved the excelsior banner—though never, I'm proud to say, the bloody shirt. And look how far this got the *Tribune!*

I'm told that even so, they're putting out a great, compendious paper these days over at the *Times*. Then you put out an even greater one that isn't compendious. Publish a Sunday edition that people not only can read but actually lift. Let the *Times* people thrive by massive organization. As for you, thrive by individuals. I did, though it never made me rich.

How well I remember the day when your grandfather came into our old office on Printing House Square, young and fresh from serving Lincoln at the White House, and I hired him on the spot. I now hear it said that my memory was faulty, that I wasn't even around at the time, and that it was Managing Editor Whitelaw Reid who spotted Hay and put him on the payroll without my knowing. Legends! Have managing editors on their own ever hired poets? For your grandfather was a poet then, even though he later became a diplomat and public oracle like Reid and like yourself. I can still see him bouncing around the city room declaiming his "Pike County Ballads" before we published them, and taking my reporters into O'Leary's bar across the street to help them learn by heart:

> *Whar have you been for the last three year*
> *That you haven't heard folks tell*
> *How Jimmy Bludso passed in his checks*
> *The night of the Prairie Belle . . .*

Jock, my son, begin by hiring poets—even like your grandfather. Newspapering was always too threatened by prose. Hire dreamers, hire mavericks, hire what you today call odd-balls. Look at whom *I* hired: young Charles A. Dana, for instance, fresh from Brook Farm as a wide-eyed young socialist—though he soon became a staunch Republican like myself. Or Mark Twain before he had become known by that name, and young Henry Villard before he ever dreamed of building Pacific railroads, and Margaret Fuller, who brought her teachings about Emancipated Woman right into my own home. I sent Bayard Taylor—another poet—with Perry to Japan, and for covering European revolutions I hired a fellow with special inside knowledge: Karl Marx.

Did I agree with all they said in the *Tribune*, or did they necessarily with me? Of course not. Often I didn't agree even with myself. I think Walt Whitman had the word for it: "Do I contradict myself? Very well then, I contradict myself. I am large, I contain multitudes." But I think the best way to contain multitudes is to spot their differences, not just their lowest common denominator. Every man worth knowing is at some time an inquiring rebel or renegade at heart. So take my advice, young Jock: entertain rebels—particularly Republican rebels, if you can find 'em—just so long as they have a cause. In fact, have many causes. In my day I had Fourierism and vegetarianism and temperance and Graham bread and land reform and female rights and Negro emancipation, up to the point at which my *Tribune* was nicknamed America's "G.M.O."—Great Moral Organ. I'm not saying you should come out for Graham bread. But I hope you'll do more than simply endorse the constituted civic deities and their toothpastes. Few of them really scour and clean.

Ah, even if you follow my advice, you will make mistakes. Look at some of my own: In 1860, my first choice for President was not Abraham Lincoln but Edward Bates, and in 1864, again not Lincoln but General Rosecrans. Worst of all, my choice for President in '72 was Horace Greeley, when I should have been content to remain simply the editor of the New York *Tribune*.

Don't repeat my blunders; yet don't be afraid of my example. I speak to you over a long distance, yet there's a sort of bond between us. I came in when the American newspaper was still young and just rising; you come in when many say it is threatened with decline. Are you going to tell me you suffer from competition at the hands of other forms of communication and mass entertainment? In my time I had such competition, too—in the form of shows like those put on by my earthy friends Phineas T. Barnum and the Reverend Henry Ward Beecher. There is this difference, I'll grant. Barnum's circuses and Beecher's sanctimonious sermons assumed that the public knew little and suspected less. I gather that in your day their successor, Madison Avenue, assumes that although the public now knows, it doesn't really care and is too dull to discriminate in any case. Yet amid this final insult to the general intelligence, do not despair, my friend. In fact, be of good cheer! The public *does* discriminate, when given a chance. Look (though it hurts me to say this) down the street at the New York *Times!*

And what is this "public" they speak of? It hasn't changed; it's still composed of individuals, Jock. The best publisher and editor, I have always thought, is the one who doesn't care one hoot what his "public" supposedly thinks en masse, but who cares passionately for what he himself and those whom he most likes and trusts believe. You have been an ambassador abroad, and I guess you know that the strongest ambassador anywhere is the one who speaks his mind clearly and firmly. Be such an ambassador to our people at home. Don't dress up for the part; yet don't dress down, either. Trust in yourself above all; dare to be different. I greet over the years the editors of the rival New York *Times*, who sometimes do dare, despite all that money of theirs. But I greet particularly yourself, who must dare. Come West, young man, and help open up the country!

ICI ORIE DEX CIET ET TERRE SOLEIL EC LVNE ET COZ ELEMEN

NATIONALBIBLIOTHEK, VIENNA

SPACE AND THE SPIRIT OF MAN

Out among the stars, in his conquest of space, man

may learn whether the universe has a plan or purpose

By ARTHUR C. CLARKE

Astronomy is the oldest of the sciences and the one that has not only the widest popular appeal but also the most profound philosophical implications. This was never more true than at the present time, when the horizons of human knowledge are not so much expanding as exploding. New discoveries and techniques—such as the development of electronic instruments, the launching of artificial satellites, the detection of radio waves from space—have invigorated the whole science and shed new light on problems over which men have argued in vain for centuries.

Yet what has already happened is merely the prelude to far more startling events, for no well-informed person now doubts that the conquest of interplanetary space, first by instrument-carrying rockets and later by manned vehicles, is now about to begin. In a period that will be very short by the standards of history—perhaps a century at the most —we may have established physical contact with all the major solid bodies in our solar system. A landing on the remotest of the sun's planets may now be nearer to us in time than the Battle of Gettysburg.

The shadow of these coming events already lies across our

As Aristotle wrote, all men begin "by wondering that things are as they are." This representation of the Creator measuring the world comes from a thirteenth-century illuminated French manuscript.

age, stirring the thoughts of all men who have ever stared at the night sky and wondered what part our species is destined to play in the unfolding drama of the universe. Many of the great questions of religion and philosophy must now be reformulated, and there is more than a possibility that some which seemed forever beyond hope of solution may soon be answered.

Whether intelligent life exists outside the Earth is, perhaps, unique among these problems in its intellectual and emotional appeal. The only type of life that we can imagine without losing ourselves in biological fantasies must be planet-based, and until a short time ago astronomers felt reluctantly certain that planets were exceedingly rare phenomena. Indeed, planets were regarded as the results of cosmic accidents that could occur only a very few times in the entire history of any well-conducted universe.

Today we are fairly confident that the exact reverse is true; modern theories of the formation of the solar system suggest that many, if not most, stars must have planets revolving around them. This outlook was given considerable support by the detection in 1942 of a hitherto unknown body—much too small to be a sun—in the double-star system 61 Cygni. This binary system is one of our closest neighbors; it would be a most remarkable coincidence, if planets were indeed rare, to find a specimen practically on our doorstep. If we eliminate systems that, through the instability of the central sun or for some other reason, seem unpromising as the abodes of life, we may not be far from the truth if we guess that one star in ten possesses at least one planet upon which life could theoretically exist.

This leads us to the second and equally remarkable transformation that the last ten or fifteen years have brought. As recently as 1947 it was possible for Lecomte du Noüy, in his widely read book, *Human Destiny*, to maintain that living things could not possibly arise from "dead" inorganic matter by the operation of purely natural forces. The complexity of even the simplest single-celled organism was so enormous that to expect atoms of carbon, hydrogen, oxygen, and the rest to form one by spontaneous aggregation was much less probable than that Eddington's famous army of simian typists should produce the entire works of Shakespeare at the first attempt. Life's appearance on Earth (or elsewhere) must therefore have been consciously directed and controlled by some organizing force, which it was tempting to identify as the hand of God.

We now know, thanks to the work of such biologists as Haldane and Oparin, that this apparently convincing argument is wholly fallacious, and that life can probably evolve from nonliving matter in the circumstances that must exist upon many primitive, newly formed planets. The process may, indeed, be inevitable when we are dealing with astronomical time periods; the idea that life on this planet is some kind of freak or special creation has vanished with the belief in the uniqueness of the solar system. Stanley Miller's famous experiment at the University of Chicago in 1952, in which a complex organic soup was produced by the action of electrical discharges upon simple solutions of carbon dioxide, ammonia, methane, and other gases, suggests how the first steps in the evolution of life may have taken place. (For an entertaining and not-too-technical account of the way in which the chemicals of life may build themselves up from elementary substances, see the essay "The Unblind Workings of Chance" in Dr. Isaac Asimov's book *Only a Trillion*.)

That both planets and living creatures are common throughout the universe must, therefore, now be taken as highly probable, though it cannot yet be proved beyond doubt. We may be hopelessly conservative if we guess that life may be associated with one star in every hundred. Dr. Harlow Shapley, in his book *Of Stars and Men*, reduces the figure to one in a million million by being deliberately ultrapessimistic; he considers a more reasonable estimate to be one in a million. But any figure is, at the present stage of our semi-ignorance, pure guesswork; let us for the sake of argument settle on that one in a hundred, and see where it leads us.

It implies the existence of a billion life-bearing worlds in our single galaxy—the whirlpool of stars of which our sun is an undistinguished out-of-town member, lying in one of the remoter spiral arms. And within the range of our telescopes there are approximately a billion other galaxies.

Now a billion is a number all too familiar in today's budgets and military estimates, but this does not mean that anyone can visualize it. Should you feel like trying, I recommend this simple and highly instructive experiment:

Go down to the nearest beach and collect a bucketful of sand; then bring it home and empty it on the table. You now have in front of you—assuming that the sand is of reasonable fineness—something like a billion separate particles. Sift them through your fingers; each is a distinct entity, different from all its companions. How long would it take you to examine every clearly visible individual in the quite small pile before you? Devoting one minute to each, and working eight hours a day, the project would keep you busy for almost six thousand years—the whole span of human history.

That is what a billion means; and now try to imagine that every one of those grains of sand is itself a world, perhaps teeming with life, and perhaps bearing rational creatures who measure their history not in thousands but in millions of years. If you succeed, you have a faint mental picture of our galaxy; if you wish to visualize the whole observed universe, however, the operation must be repeated with each grain of sand now representing an entire galaxy.

There is a temptation, when brainwashed by such numbers, to argue that these astronomical vistas are of no practical importance, since we can never have direct knowledge of more than a small—indeed, relatively submicroscopic— portion of the universe. A similar policy was adopted by those followers of Aristotle who refused to look through Galileo's telescope and to see for themselves that Jupiter, as well as Earth, had moons revolving round it. If they could not be seen by the naked eye, these gentlemen argued, the heretical satellites did not really exist.

However, we cannot pretend that the universe isn't there, for our own children will be starting to explore it, and even their first modest voyages will completely transform our view of the cosmos. Once we can climb the mere hundred miles or so that separate us from space, and thus establish satellite observatories beyond the murk and haze of the atmosphere, it will be like emerging from a fog into the light of day. *Without traveling any further from Earth than Washington is from*

New York, we will have broken through the vision barrier and will be able to view Mars, for example, from an apparent distance of only a few thousand miles. With the telescopes that we will be able to construct and operate under the perfect seeing conditions in space, we may even be able to look for the planets of other suns.

It is obviously impossible to anticipate the discoveries which will be made when we succeed in escaping from Earth; indeed, one characteristic of most really important discoveries is their unexpectedness. At the moment the astronomical evidence suggests that we will find some sort of life in the solar system (on Mars, almost certainly; on Venus, just possibly) but that we will not encounter intelligence. It would be rather too much to hope that two intelligent species should exist in the same small region of space and at the same moment of time.

The discovery of any form of life, however humble, on the planets would greatly affect our outlook upon the universe by changing what is now a surmise into a certainty. Even a few lichens on Mars, or a few amoebae in the (still hypothetical) seas of Venus would prove that life is not a rare disease that happens to have attacked the planet Earth. And with that settled, it would be illogical to deny the existence of higher forms elsewhere.

It is just possible that we may find direct proof of this on Mars; even if we have missed the Martians by a few million years, their records will still be written in the rocks of an arid world that knows none of the erosion or the interchange of land and sea that has obliterated so much of our own planet's remote past. But all this is pure, unfounded speculation; until we have reason to believe the contrary, it would be safest to assume that Homo sapiens is the only intelligent creature yet to have evolved in the solar system. To find our equals or our peers, we must go further afield to the planets of other suns.

This, to put it mildly, presents problems. Though we are now about to challenge interplanetary distances, the gulfs separating us from the stars are a million times greater, and light itself takes years to span them. Nevertheless, there are good reasons for thinking that interstellar travel will ultimately be possible. When we have developed really efficient nuclear propulsion devices, speeds comparable to that of light should be attainable, and round trips to the nearer stars would take about ten years. Though tedious, this would not be out of the question even for manned vessels; such techniques as suspended animation, or the use of purely automatic exploring vessels, would extend this range indefinitely.

Nor need *physical* transportation be necessary. With today's electronic techniques, stretched to the utmost, we could just about get a readable Morse signal to the nearest star. It might therefore be worthwhile, as soon as we can establish satellite listening posts well away from the radio racket and electrical interference of Earth, to begin a search

Hindus saw the universe girdled by a cobra. A flat earth and its candle-like sun are held up by four elephants (the compass points), atop a giant turtle in a sea of milk.

Ancient Egyptians believed the barge of the sun journeyed across the arched back of the sky goddess Nut, who was supported by the god of air and the earth god Geb, below.

According to Balinese mythology, eclipses occur when the bodyless head of Kala Ruhu swallows the moon or the sun. Here the demon has devoured a seemingly unconcerned moon.

for intelligently modulated signals from space. If we can tackle interstellar communication only sixty years after we have invented radio, it is not unreasonable to assume that there may be transmitters within a few light-years of us far more powerful than any we have yet built. Even today, many of our radars must far outrange the solar system—though we can be thankful that all our commercial radio programs will have faded far below the level of cosmic noise before they can affront any stellar neighbors.

By one means or another, therefore, we may hope to establish the existence of extraterrestrial intelligences before many more decades—or at most, centuries—have passed. If anyone still feels doubtful of this, I would remind him of the unfortunate error of Auguste Comte, who rashly proclaimed our eternal ignorance concerning the composition of the stars. The speed and thoroughness with which the spectroscope refuted him is a good reminder that there are no apparently fundamental limits to knowledge that may not be transcended by new techniques or inventions.

Keeping this in mind, it is not premature, and it is certainly stimulating, to consider what effect these undoubted but still unknown revelations will have upon the minds of men. They will certainly accelerate a process which has been gaining momentum since Copernicus dethroned the Earth from the center of creation and started it upon its still-continuing journey to the periphery of the universe. Today, it is difficult for us to believe that as recently as the time of Shakespeare no one knew that other worlds existed. Though the Greeks had surmised it, there was no direct proof until the invention of the telescope *circa* 1608, and so to almost all educated men up to a dozen generations ago, our planet *was* the universe. One might even say that this was still true for 90 per cent of the human race until October 4, 1957.

The expansion of the time scale has had equally striking effects on human thought. Until well into the last century much of the Western world believed in the literal truth of

CONTINUED ON PAGE 122

Although not all the planets shown in this eighteenth-century chart were known to Nicolaus Copernicus, the Polish father of modern astronomy, the plan is based on his great work, De Revolutionibus Orbium Coelestium, *published in 1543. He demonstrated that the earth rotates daily on its axis and that earth and planets (shown inside the ring of zodiacal symbols) revolve in orbits around the sun. At the upper left, the chart-maker has compared the size of the planets to that of the sun, and below this are sketches of Mars, Venus, and Mercury as they appear when nearest and farthest from the earth. At bottom left, flanked by cherubs playing with telescopes and a large quadrant, is a representation of the solar eclipse of May 12, 1706. The three green circles at lower right illustrate the Ptolemaic, Tychonic (after Tycho Brahe), and Copernican systems. At right center is a drawing of a lunar eclipse, and above it, amid the clouds, yellow, target-like figures indicating that other stars in the firmament have planetary systems similar to our own.*

30

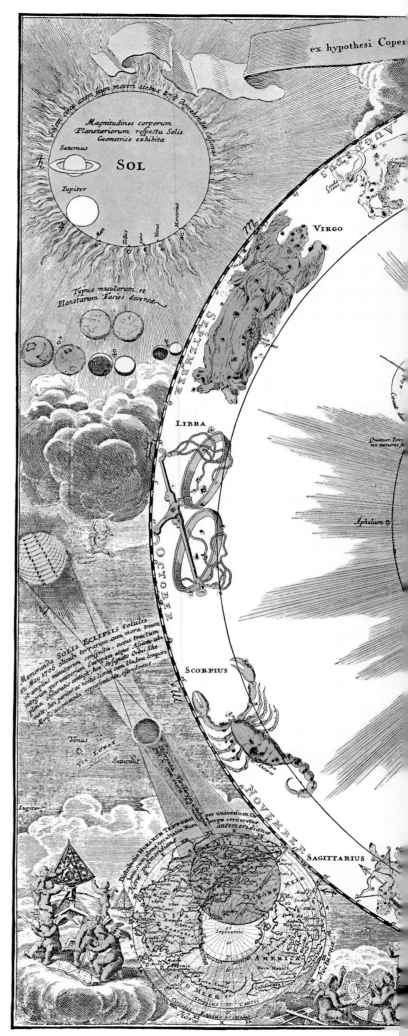

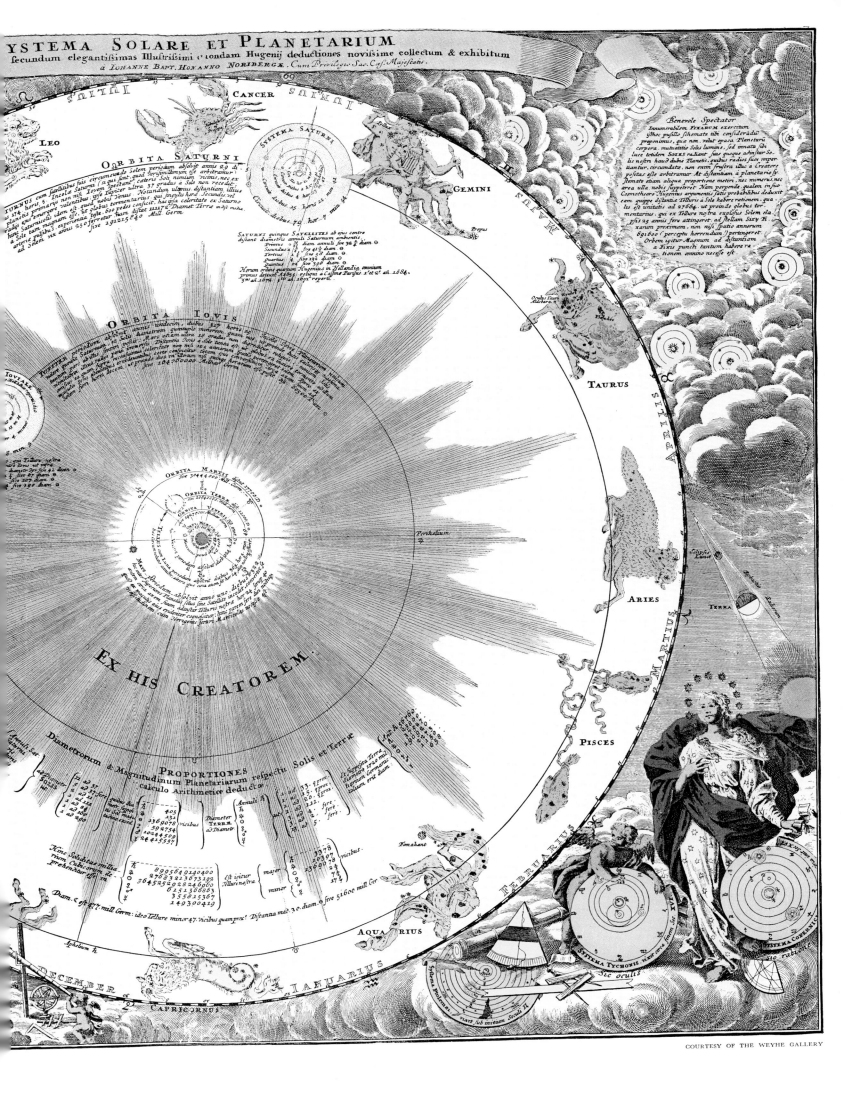

YSTEMA SOLARE ET PLANETARIUM

secundum elegantissimas Illustrissimi quondam Hugenij deductiones novissime collectum & exhibitum
a IOHANNE BAPT. HOMANNO NORIBERGÆ. Cum Privilegio Sac. Cæs. Majestatis.

EX HIS CREATOREM.

PROPORTIONES

At Millwall in 1858 the pioneer of modern engineering, clad in the vestments of early Victorian England, stands before the anchor chains of his last and proudest work, the steamship Great Eastern.

By L. T. C. ROLT

THE GREAT ENGINEER

Isambard Kingdom Brunel

More than a century ago, in early Victorian England, he built the longest

bridge, the fastest railway, and the biggest ship the world had ever seen

In the library of Bristol University there is preserved a remarkable series of sketchbooks. Their assured draftsmanship proclaims them the work of an artist, but what is really remarkable about them is the astonishing range of subjects portrayed: steamships, locomotives, pieces of mechanism, plans and elevations of railway stations and other buildings, tunnel portals and bridges of masonry or iron. It is evident that their author was not only an artist but a civil engineer, a mechanical engineer, and, not least, an architect who was the master of a dozen different architectural styles that he delighted in adapting to new and novel purposes. Occasionally, hastily scribbled notes appear that are no less remarkable than the drawings. Thus, beside a sketch of a ship's hull, the artist has written: "Say 600 ft x 65 ft x 30 ft"—grandiose dimensions that make it difficult for us to credit the penciled date: "March 25th, 1852."

We should be right in thinking that a genius of no mean order had been at work between the covers of these books, for the artist was Isambard Kingdom Brunel, a man who was not only one of the greatest engineers in history but one of the most versatile and dynamic personalities the modern world has known. His sketches, many of them no more than the doodles of a restless imagination throwing off ideas like sparks, were destined to be translated, by dint of the blood and the sweat of thousands of men and the expenditure of

millions of pounds, into material achievements that astonished the world: a great railway system on which mile-a-minute speeds were achieved for the first time; three steamships, each in turn the largest ever built, one of which established the first regular transatlantic steamer service.

Brunel, one feels, was one of those rare mortals who could have excelled in any calling he chose to pursue. He pursued engineering as his profession because in early nineteenth-century England it offered him the most satisfying outlet for his prodigious creative powers. It is significant that his most intimate friend was not a fellow engineer but his artist brother-in-law John Horsley. Horsley knew nothing of engineering and said that what he loved in Brunel was his high courage and his artistic gifts—his love of painting, music, and drama.

Brunel himself confessed that as a youth he was forever dreaming of ambitious schemes, castles in Spain as he called them. But to have ideas, however brilliant, is one thing; to translate them into practice is quite another, and an imaginative genius often lacks the ability to concentrate upon detail and the capacity for sheer hard work that are essential before ideas can take practical shape. It was the secret of Brunel's success that he was able to do both these things. His sketchbooks reveal the meticulous attention to detail that tempered the heat of his inspiration. We notice how

33

In the half-completed Thames Tunnel in 1827, Isambard Brunel held a banquet to celebrate the completion of repairs after a cave-in. In this painting he rises at left to propose a toast to his father, Sir Marc Brunel, who was the chief proponent and designer of the tunnel.

even the most hasty sketch is drawn upon squared paper so that, if the idea seemed promising, it could be more readily translated into a precisely dimensioned drawing. We may notice, too, how each book has two strips of glass paper—coarse and fine—pasted on the inside cover so that the fine point of Brunel's pencil could always be quickly sharpened to follow his inspiration.

In whatever task he undertook, Brunel insisted upon his absolute personal responsibility. When the directors of the Great Western Railway reprimanded one of Brunel's assistant engineers, they received this stinging retort: "I will do my best to keep my team in order, but I cannot do it if the master sits by me and amuses himself by touching them up with the whip." That he was indeed well able to keep his team in order, this letter to an erring assistant shows:

Plain gentlemanly language seems to have no effect upon you. I must try stronger language and stronger measures. You are a cursed, lazy, inattentive, apathetic vagabond, and if you continue

to neglect my instructions and to show such infernal laziness, I shall send you about your business. I have frequently told you, amongst other absurd, untidy habits, that that of making drawings on the backs of others was inconvenient; by your cursed neglect of that you have again wasted more of my time than your whole life is worth, in looking for the altered drawings you were to make of the station—they wont do.

Finally, here is Brunel's working philosophy as expressed in a letter to a defeatist colleague:

You have failed, I think . . . from that which causes nine-tenths of all failures in this world, from not doing quite enough. . . . I would only impress upon you one principle of action which I have always found very successful, which is to stick obstinately to one plan (until I believe it wrong) . . . and, on the same principle, to stick to one method and push that to the utmost limits before I allow myself to wander into others; in fact, to use a simile, to stick to one point of attack, however defended, and if the force first brought up is not sufficient, to bring ten times as much; but never to try back upon another in the hope of finding it easier.

Brunel held courageously to this principle of action throughout a comparatively brief career, checkered by failure as well as triumph, in which he took the engineering world of his day by storm. Having once decided that a scheme was correct in principle, he would pursue it regardless of commercial considerations, while a single-minded quest for perfection frequently led him to ask too much of the men and the machines under his command. To put it simply, he set his sights too high, and it was this fault that drove him to his tragic death when he was at the height of his career.

Brunel's father was Sir Marc Isambard Brunel, a Frenchman of yeoman stock, whose royalist sympathies forced him to emigrate, first to New York and later to England where he married an English girl, Sophia Kingdom. Marc Brunel himself achieved considerable fame as an engineer, and at the time his only son was born at Portsea on April 9, 1806, he was installing some ingenious machines of his own design at Portsmouth Dockyard. He was thus able to give young Isambard an excellent early training and to send him to France to complete his education.

When Brunel returned to England to assist his father, it was not long before he was given the chance to prove his mettle. At the age of twenty he was appointed resident engineer of his father's last great engineering undertaking, the boring of a tunnel under the Thames from Rotherhithe to Wapping. The work was fraught with every kind of difficulty and danger. It was not only the first underwater tunnel in the world, except for certain mine workings, it was also the first in which a tunneling shield, designed by Marc Brunel, was used to protect the excavators. The miners worked in a series of cells within massive cast-iron frames, which were moved forward by jackscrew as the excavation proceeded. On a staging behind these frames the bricklayers worked, so that the brick lining of the tunnel closely followed the tail of the advancing shield.

After making trial borings, the geologists assured the Brunels that if they drove their tunnel at a certain level they would encounter only the stiff London clay. This prediction proved hopelessly wrong. As the excavation advanced under the river, the Brunels soon realized that instead of solid clay, only a few feet of gravel and mud lay between the top of the shield and the river bed. Even the shield could not ensure safety under such conditions. But although the Brunels knew full well the appalling risk they were running, the work went on. The fact that the Tunnel Company, against their advice, insisted upon admitting sight-seers to the tunnel at a shilling a time did not lighten their anxiety. "Notwithstanding every prudence on our part," wrote Marc Brunel in his diary on May 13, 1827, "a disaster may still occur. May it not be when the arch is full of visitors." Five days later the river broke in.

Young Brunel was on the surface by the head of the Rotherhithe shaft when he heard the sudden thunder of water from below and knew that the worst had happened. Soon the half-drowned miners were scrambling up the shaft stairs. Brunel shouted to them to hurry, and scarcely had the last man reached the top before a great wave carried away the stairs. It was then realized that an old man named Tillet, who looked after the pumps at the shaft bottom, was still below. Brunel seized a rope, secured one end round his waist, and slid down one of the shaft tie rods into the darkness of the drowned tunnel. Miraculously, he found the old man struggling in the water and managed to tie the rope round his waist. When rescuer and rescued had been hauled to the surface a roll call was held. No one was missing. Next day Brunel had himself lowered in a diving bell to the bed of the Thames to inspect the damage. He never wasted time.

When the hole in the river bed had been plugged with bags of clay and the workings laboriously cleared of water and silt, Brunel celebrated this victory in characteristic fashion by inviting his father and fifty of his friends to a banquet in the tunnel, at which music was provided by the band of the Coldstream Guards. This triumph was short-lived, for two months later the tunnel was drowned again.

On this occasion Brunel was in the tunnel and only escaped death by a miracle. He was working with two miners named Ball and Collins in Number One frame of the shield when the river burst in with such force that all three were swept back out of the frame into the tunnel. The bricklayers' staging was carried away, and as the water swept over him, Brunel realized that his leg was pinioned by a section of heavy timbering. By a tremendous effort he managed to free himself, but having done so, instead of immediately making for safety, this extraordinary young man stopped to gaze in admiration at the spectacle of the water pouring in. "While standing there," he wrote afterward in his private journal, "the effect was *grand*—the roar of the rushing water in a

Two months after the banquet, the walls of the tube again burst under the weight of water and of visitors to the project, and the inundation, shown in this painting by Goodall, took the lives of six workmen. Today the tunnel is part of London's subway system.

confined passage, and by its velocity rushing past the opening was grand, *very grand*. I cannot compare it to anything, cannon can be nothing to it. . . . The sight and the whole affair was well worth the risk and I would willingly pay my share, £50 about, of the expenses of such a 'spectacle.' " Brunel then turned and made for the shaft stairs, but before he could reach them he was swept off his feet and overwhelmed by an immense wave of water. This demolished the stairs and carried Ball, Collins, and four other miners to their death, but it miraculously lifted a semiconscious Brunel to the lip of the shaft.

As a consequence of this second disaster, work on the tunnel was suspended for lack of capital. It was not begun again until 1835, and it was not until 1841 that Marc Brunel saw his work completed and was rewarded with a knighthood by his Queen. In this second act of the tunnel drama the younger Brunel played no part. The chief engineer of the Great Western Railway had other work to do.

It was found that Brunel had not only damaged his leg in the tunnel but had suffered severe internal injuries, which kept him to his bed for many weeks. When he had recovered sufficiently his parents sent him to Clifton, near Bristol in the west of England, to convalesce. This chance decision was to set the course of their son's future career.

The citizens of Bristol had decided that a bridge should be built over the deep and narrow gorge of the Avon River at Clifton, and the committee in charge had announced a competition for the best design. This was just the kind of dramatic project to appeal to Brunel's imagination, and the fruits of his convalescence were three designs for suspension bridges of spans varying from 870 feet to 916 feet, which would spring from lip to lip of the gorge.

To judge their competition, the Clifton Bridge Committee appointed the most eminent civil engineer of the day, Thomas Telford. Among many great engineering achievements, Telford had been responsible for what was then the largest suspension bridge in the world, his famous bridge over the Straits of Menai, in North Wales. But Telford had grown old and cautious. Unmindful of the fact that he had once designed a bridge for the Mersey at Runcorn with a span of 1,000 feet, Telford expressed the opinion that the 600-foot span of his Menai bridge could not be exceeded

Brunel himself painted this water color of the Clifton Bridge, which he called "my first child, my darling," and which established his fame as an engineer. Brunel's design was opposed by the greatest civil engineer of the day, Sir Thomas Telford, who thought so long a bridge might collapse and wanted to support it with Gothic towers. Spanning the Avon River, it still carries the main line of British Railways west of London.

with safety, and on this score he rejected all the competing designs. He then prepared a design himself in which he reduced the span by carrying up two immense piers from the floor of the gorge. At first this design was acclaimed, but Brunel poured such scorn upon its timidity that enthusiasm waned, and ultimately it was decided to hold a second competition. In this Telford's design was rejected while Brunel's was accepted, and he was appointed engineer to the bridge committee.

Unfortunately, owing to lack of capital Brunel's splendid bridge—"my first child, my darling," as he called it—was not completed until after his death. Nevertheless this under-

taking, and the works he undertook for the Bristol Dock Company, earned him a high reputation in Bristol. Consequently, when a group of Bristol merchants were planning a railway from Bristol to London in 1833 and wanted an engineer to carry out a survey, Brunel's was among the names put forward. He realized that this was his first great chance. Railway construction offered a boundless field of opportunity for an ambitious young engineer; but at this time the infant profession was practically a monopoly of the inventive Stephensons—George and Robert—and the engineers they had trained. Yet it was characteristic of Brunel that even with this golden opportunity dangled before him, he scorned to trim his sails to the wind. The railway committee announced that the post of engineer would go to the surveyor who undertook to survey the cheapest route. Brunel replied that he would undertake to survey only one route from Bristol to London and this would be not the cheapest but the best. He got the job, but only—as he learned afterward—by one vote.

In the opinion of many people the construction of 118 miles of railway was wildly overambitious; yet Brunel saw it as only a small beginning. In imagination he was already far ahead. Before even a sod had been cut he could see his iron road monopolizing the traffic of the west of England, stretching away through Somerset and Devon into Cornwall and along the seaboard of South Wales. So it was not as the "London & Bristol" but as the Great Western Railway that the company was incorporated.

"I am Engineer to the finest work in England," Brunel wrote in his diary after his appointment, for he had resolved to make it so. Thinking of speeds that no one had so far dared to contemplate, he laid out a superbly straight and level road, spanned the Thames at Maidenhead with two of the largest and flattest arches ever built, and drove a tunnel nearly two miles long under Box Hill near Bath. Contemporaries called the tunnel project "monstrous and extraordinary, most dangerous and impracticable"; yet it was completed in just over four and a half years. Thirty million bricks were used for its lining, and a ton of candles and a ton of gun powder per week were consumed during construction. As for the bridge at Maidenhead, its collapse under the first featherweight train was confidently predicted, but it stands fast under the main line of traffic today.

Yet the controversy that these works provoked was a gentle breeze compared to the fury of the storm that raged around Brunel when he calmly announced his intention of laying his road to a rail gauge of seven feet. The Stephensons had already standardized the gauge of 4 feet 8½ inches for no better reason, as Robert Stephenson admitted, than that they had used it before on the colliery lines of the north, which followed the tracks of the ancient wagonways. Here was a precedent that Brunel unhesitatingly threw overboard. This narrow, arbitrary "coal-waggon gauge" would never do for the speeds he contemplated on his splendid road. He wanted greater stability, and he wanted to give locomotive designers more elbow room when planning the engines to give him the speed. It is a measure of the force and the magic of Brunel's personality that in the face of the bitterest opposition from every railway engineer in the country he managed to carry his directors with him, and the broad gauge metals went down.

Brunel argued that in practice the advantages of his broad gauge would prove so overwhelming that other railway companies would be forced to change to it. Had he been earlier in the field he might have been right, but the smaller Standard gauge was already too firmly established,

The building of the Great Western Railway from London to Bristol absorbed Brunel's prodigious energies from 1833 to 1841. Between Chippenham and Bath the Box Tunnel (above)

and commercially the broad gauge proved a costly mistake although it was not finally banished from Brunel's main line until 1892. As an engineering tour de force the broad gauge accomplished all that Brunel claimed for it. Under the driving inspiration of his locomotive superintendent, Daniel Gooch, the Swindon shops built in thirteen weeks the *Great Western*, a locomotive with single driving wheels eight feet in diameter and a boiler of unprecedented size. At this time (1846) an average speed of 35 mph was considered fast going on the Standard gauge; yet within a month of leaving the shops, the *Great Western* had reeled off the 194 miles from Paddington to Exeter in 208 minutes, and with 100 tons behind her had covered the 77½ miles from London to Swindon in 78 minutes start to stop. She was the first of a long line of broad gauge flyers that carried no numbers, only the proudest of names: *Iron Duke*, *Great Britain*, *Lightning*, *Emperor*, *Pasha*, *Sultan*, *Lord of the Isles*. These were the locomotives that hauled the first express trains in the world, trains which themselves acquired names that were to become immortal: *The Cornishman*, *The Flying Dutchman*, and *The Zulu*.

George Stephenson called Brunel's broad gauge a humbug, and the victory was ultimately his, but if it accomplished nothing else, the example of the broad gauge acted as a tremendous stimulus to railway development by breaking the Stephenson monopoly.

Brunel's extension of his broad gauge road westward through Devon and Cornwall followed the same checkered pattern of previous successes and failures. On the South Devon Railway west of Exeter he tried out what was called the "atmospheric" system of traction. A continuous pipeline was laid between the rails, and instead of a locomotive, the trains were headed by a special carriage equipped with a piston that ran in the pipe. A series of pumping stations at three-mile intervals beside the line exhausted the air from the pipe so that the trains were driven along by the pressure of the atmosphere acting upon the traveling piston. This arrangement worked very well for a time, but then a series of troubles developed and the scheme ended in costly failure.

Once he had become convinced that the system was unworkable, Brunel had the courage to urge its immediate abandonment even though a majority of the directors of the railway company were in favor of continuing the experiment. Had he taken the easier course of siding with them in some futile effort to save face, his railway career might well have ended ignominiously, at least so far as the west country was concerned. As it was, confidence in his abilities remained unshaken, and he was able to carry the broad gauge metals through Cornwall to their terminus at Penzance. The last link to be forged on this long rail route from London was Brunel's famous Royal Albert Bridge over the Tamar at Saltash. This great bridge, Brunel's final masterpiece of railway engineering, stands today as his memorial. For in May, 1859, when the Prince Consort opened the

had to be carved through almost two miles of hilly country, much of it solid rock. The tracks were laid (below) on a route that Brunel insisted should be not the cheapest or easiest but the best.

bridge, and the long road from London to Penzance was complete, Brunel had only four months to live. It was from a couch carried on a platform truck that the dying engineer saw his finished work for the first and last time.

In all, about 2,000 miles of railway were built under Brunel's direction. This, one might suppose, would be more than enough for one short lifetime, but in fact it was only half of Brunel's activities. In the world of marine engineering he made a mark that was even more sensational than his broad gauge railways.

This story began at an early board meeting of the Great Western Railway Company when someone expressed misgivings as to the length of the proposed line from London to Bristol. "Why not make it longer," suggested Brunel through the smoke of his cigar, "and have a steamboat go from Bristol to New York and call it the *Great Western?*" Those staid frock-coated gentlemen of the board accepted this sally as one of their engineer's characteristic little jokes, but that it was no joke they soon realized when a company was formed in Bristol, which began building the *Great Western*, the largest steamship in the world at the time. Once again the prophets of disaster gathered like ravens. It could be proved by calculation, they croaked, that no steamship could carry enough coal for an Atlantic crossing under continuous power. But Brunel realized that they had got their figures wrong; that whereas the carrying capacity of a hull increases as the cube of its dimensions, its area, or, in other words, the power needed to drive it through the water, only increases as the square of those dimensions. Hence, the larger the ship the greater its cruising range without refueling. This was the simple proposition which inspired Brunel to build his first ship.

As the *Great Western*, a wooden paddler with a displacement of 2,300 tons, took shape, established shipping interests began to wonder uneasily about their future if Brunel's experiment came off. To be on the safe side the British & American Steam Navigation Company of London laid down the *British Queen* on the Thames at Limehouse. But this ship was still far from completion when the *Great Western* arrived in London under sail to take on her engines at Blackwall. Determined to steal Brunel's thunder if it could, the rival company thereupon chartered the little Irish steam packet *Sirius* and began to fit her out for an Atlantic voyage. The *Sirius* narrowly won the race to get the two ships ready for sea. She sailed from the Thames March 28, 1838. With Brunel on board, the *Great Western* followed

The Great Western passing Portishead

As had often been the case, Brunel was forced to fight both hardened convention and physical danger in the completion of the Great Western. *Engineers of the early nineteenth century had an inherited pessimism about transoceanic travel by steamship, on the grounds that no vessel could carry enough fuel. On her maiden voyage the* Great Western *proved them wrong.*

Less than two hours out of the Thames at the beginning of its race, the Great Western *caught fire, and Brunel, pitched down a ladder, barely escaped death in the flooded boiler room. The ship made port at Bristol, and the indefatigable Brunel supervised repairs from his sickbed. This water color shows the* Great Western *passing Portishead on the English coast, near Bristol.*

on March 31, bound for Bristol to take on passengers. Knowing that the master of the *Sirius* intended coaling at Cork, Brunel was not unduly worried by the starting handicap until, before his splendid ship had cleared the Thames estuary, smoke and flames suddenly belched from her boiler room. The boiler lagging round the base of the funnel had ignited and set fire to the deck planking. Fortunately the outbreak was mastered before any serious damage was done, but it nearly cost Brunel his life. As he was fighting the flames, the charred rung of a ladder collapsed under him and he fell eighteen feet onto the boiler room plating where, knocked unconscious, he nearly drowned in the water that had collected there. In great pain, he was rowed ashore to the care of a cottager on Canvey Island, while on his insistence the *Great Western* put out to sea after a delay of twelve hours.

It seemed that the result of the race must be a foregone conclusion, for whereas the *Sirius* left Cork on April 4, four precious days elapsed before the *Great Western* got away from the more distant port of Bristol. The little *Sirius* docked in New York after nineteen days at sea, on the morning of April 23. It had been a close call, for her coal bunkers were empty and she had had to burn barrels of resin from her cargo. A few hours later New York realized how close a race the little *Sirius* had run, for on that same historic morning of St. George's Day the *Great Western* dropped her anchor off Sandy Hook fifteen days and five hours from the Port of Bristol. James Gordon Bennett graphically described the scene for his morning *Herald* readers when the *Great Western* arrived in New York: "The sky was clear—the crowds immense. The Battery was filled with the human multitude. . . . Below, on the broad, blue water, appeared this huge thing of life, with four masts and emitting volumes of smoke. She looked black and blackguard . . . rakish, cool, reckless, fierce and forbidding in sombre colors to an extreme. As she neared the *Sirius*, she slackened her movements and took a sweep round, forming a sort of half circle. At this moment the whole Battery sent forth a tumultuous shout of delight at the revelation of her magnificent proportions. After making another turn towards Staten Island, she made another sweep and shot towards the East River with extraordinary speed. The vast multitude rent the air with their shouts again, waving handkerchiefs, hats, hurrahing!" But these enthusiastic New Yorkers could not then appreciate the really vital point about this demonstration; this was that the *Great Western* still had 200 tons of coal in her bunkers. In that fact, Brunel had triumphantly

The Great Britain *(right), second of Brunel's giant vessels and the first iron-hulled, screw-propelled ship to cross any ocean, was launched at Bristol in 1843 before the gala crowds shown in this lithograph.*

proved the practicability of transatlantic steam navigation.

The *Great Western* was a complete success and most truly earned the honor of the Atlantic Blue Riband, which she was the first ship to wear, by making no less than 67 crossings in eight years. Her best records were thirteen days westbound and twelve days, six hours eastbound. She was followed on the Atlantic run in 1845 by Brunel's second ship, the *Great Britain*, which like her predecessor was the biggest ship afloat when she was launched. Apart from her size, the *Great Britain* was the first iron steamer and the first screw-propelled ship to cross any ocean. It is doubtful whether any other man would have had the courage to embody two such revolutionary innovations in one design.

As though to chasten his presumption, ill fortune seemed to dog Brunel and his creations, and the *Great Britain* was no exception to this rule. On September 22, 1846, the ship left Liverpool for New York with 180 passengers on board —the largest complement ever to sail in a transatlantic steamer up to that time. A few hours later she had run aground in Dundrum Bay on the coast of Northern Ireland due to a faulty chart and compass deflection caused by the iron hull. Grinding over rocks on an exposed shore, the *Great Britain* successfully withstood a battering that would have broken up any other ship afloat, and all her passengers were safely landed. The next spring, under Brunel's direction, she was successfully salvaged. The *Great Britain* continued to trade until 1886, and even now the remains of her almost indestructible hull can still be seen in Sparrow Cove, Falkland Islands. CONTINUED ON PAGE 136

The 320,000-ton Great Eastern, *first called the* Leviathan, *is shown below under construction at Millwall. Ironically, Brunel's grandiose vision turned on him, and the huge ship was later rendered obsolete for its proposed service in Australia passenger trade because it was too large to pass through the new Suez Canal.*

42

Like his two previous ships, the Great Eastern *(left) was the largest of its time, and like the others, it experienced a streak of bad luck. An explosion caused heavy damage on its maiden voyage, and news of this misfortune was a crushing blow to the mortally ill Brunel.*

43

By GILBERT HIGHET

THE MYSTERY OF MAD MAGGIE

A new interpretation of one of the strangest paintings in art history

I have always enjoyed paintings and other portrayals of hell and devils and the torments of the damned. This is the result of a good Scottish Presbyterian upbringing. No cosier way of spending a wet Sunday afternoon in Scotland can be devised than examining (with a magnifying glass if necessary) several dozen horrifying pictures showing the separating of the sheep from the goats and the carrying of the condemned down into hell, and the varieties of their tortures, infinite in ingenuity, infinite in pain, infinite in time. Most of the devils I studied when I was young were comparatively modern in face and figure. Those by Gustave Doré are typical: anatomically they are men, with noble and strong torsos and limbs; only the addition of big bat wings and long snaky tails, together with a savage, rather Mongolian expression, tells us that they are demons of the pit. Doré and other artists like him conceived the devils as angels, fallen.

But evil ought to be more repulsive, more terrifying. It ought not to be good misplaced and misapplied, but the very reverse of good: unrecognizable even as virtue perverted. Therefore the only portrayals of hell and the devils which now seem to me to be satisfactory are certain Oriental pictures and sculptures, particularly from Tibet, and the paintings of Pieter Bruegel and his master, Hieronymus Bosch. These were two Flemish artists who lived and worked between 1460 and 1570; they did not know each other, but Bruegel got much of his training from copying the brilliant paintings and engravings of Bosch and adapted many of Bosch's mysterious ideas.

Both Bruegel and Bosch have several pictures showing hell or the activities of the fiends: devils tempt St. Anthony, haunt the bedside of a dying miser, or carouse in a mindless hell of lust and vapidity. But the strangest of all their infernal pictures is a surrealist masterpiece by Bruegel. It has haunted me for many years; although I have never seen it (it is in a little collection in Antwerp), I have studied reproductions of it; I have thought about it and compared it

with other paintings by these two Flemish mystics; and I am beginning to understand it.

It is a big picture, about five feet by four, painted on a wooden panel, not in oil, but with mineral colors mixed with egg. It bears no name, and only traces of Bruegel's signature are still visible; but we know the name which it acquired because the earliest historian of Flemish painting, Carel van Mander, writing one generation after it was painted, calls it *Dulle Griet*, which means "Mad Maggie." The picture must take its name from the central figure, which is that of a woman. She is a slender woman in her middle forties, wearing ordinary clothes: dark shoes and stockings, a white blouse, or shift, an overdress of neutral gray, and a black jacket with red and black sleeves. But over that she is wearing some of a soldier's armor: a steel breastplate, one huge metal gauntlet, a metal helmet; in her right hand she carries a strong sword. Her eyes are wide open, staring in some excited intensity; her hair is unbound and streams behind her; her face is thin and haggard, with a pointed nose and wrinkles of tension around her toothless mouth and on her drawn jaw and neck; her lips are parted, either in eagerness or in the beginning of a shriek. She is a woman who has turned into a soldier: not only that, but a conquering soldier, for she is loaded down with loot. She has a big treasure casket in the crook of her left arm; her apron, looped up below the cuirass, holds a large pitcher which may be gold; her left hand grasps some more plunder, largely household equipment; and from her breastplate dangles what is either a rich bracelet or a necklace with a watch attached to it. Wherever she has been on her expedition, she has done well.

But where has she been? For that matter, where is she now? In the first few minutes, as we look at her picture with astonished bewilderment, it is impossible for us to tell. Then we begin to understand. We start by realizing that it is not a landscape on this earth. The sky is not blue, or white, but red and black, and lit by lurid fires and striped by pillars

DETAIL (AND FULL PAINTING ON PAGES 48-49) COURTESY MUSÉE MAYER VAN DEN BERGH, ANTWERP; ANTON SCHROLL & CO., VIENNA

Dulle Griet, or Mad Maggie, is the central figure of Bruegel's painting. The whole picture, from which this detail is taken, is reproduced on pages 48-49.

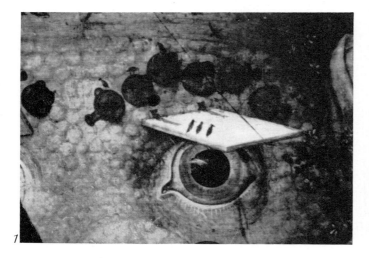

of smoke. There are a few strangely shaped trees, but no fields or signs of regular human life. A river runs across the front of the picture; yet it is not a normal river. It has been made into a moat for a strange fortification. There are bridges and drawbridges which cross it, and at right and left it disappears below two massive buildings filled with struggling figures. The building on the right is more or less normal; but that on the left—is it a building or is it a monster? Its mouth, where the water pours in, or out, is ringed with fierce teeth; its roof, after trying to be a rounded dome, finishes off in a peak like a turnip, or perhaps a foolscap; and one of its round windows has become a huge round, glaring eye (Detail 1, above). The thing is both a house and a head; it even has a nose, with a ring through it.

We are looking, then, at a region which is inhabited and fortified. Outside its walls, in the very foreground, is Mad Maggie with her sword and her armor and her loot. She is marching across a little hill, either because she has finished her work for the time being and wants to take her loot to a place of safety before returning for more, or because she is still on the warpath. Besides her, there is only one group of normal human beings in the picture. They are all women, dressed in workaday clothes; but instead of doing workaday things, they are engaged in a battle that looks like a hideous nightmare. On the right-hand bridge, and at the gate of the fortification, they are fighting and beating a group of monsters. Toadlike, apelike, swollen and twisted into shapes like distorted embryos, the monsters in vain struggle against the women, who slap them and buffet them and thrust them aside and trample them underfoot (Detail 2); and see, the women have broken down the door of the fortress, they have crowded their way inside, and they are coming out laden with booty, like Mad Maggie herself. Two of them carry sacks full of household plunder; one has a soup caldron on her head because her arms are full; the women emerge in triumph, while more monsters vainly attempt to rally the forces of whatever obscene power inhabits those grim walls. At the other side of the picture, within the house which is a huge face, other monsters are retreating in wild confusion, as though terror-stricken by the ferocity of Maggie and her minions. Some are plunging madly into the

moat, while two—a badger with the face of a heron, and an indeterminate creature with clawed feet and no face, who wears a helmet covering his whole body—are pulling at the drawbridge rope (Detail 3); a terrified mouse looks round it and two black lizards scamper in to safety.

The women are creatures of this earth; the monsters are not, and they do not live in the world we know. They are devils—not the suave, energetic fiends of the comparatively modern romantic age, nor the swaggering, almost human demons who mingle with mankind as Mephistopheles did, but the devils who stand for the reversal of everything that is reasonable, logical, and comprehensible; the opposites of grace both human and divine, of dignity and of nobility, and even of seemliness. The place with the fortifications around it is hell. Far in the distance, we can see the smoke of the torment which they inhabit forever. Scattered here and there are random groups of sufferers, or maniacs, wild dancers, gruesome musicians. Here there is no order, no peace, no loveliness possible. Bruegel evidently conceived hell not as like a torture chamber on this earth, but rather as the interior of the mind of a raving lunatic. Even the fortifications are absurd, broken, and capricious; since the devils, being opposed to reason and the law, cannot organize themselves (this is the conception we see in Dante's *Inferno* also), their forces are contemptible, although terrifying; random, ridiculous, although superhuman.

If we want to find the central figure, the ruler of this infernal kingdom, the devil himself, we should remember what Bruegel does in other pictures: he puts the most important figure in a position which is central, but somehow escapes the eye. Jesus on the way to his crucifixion, the bridegroom in the *Rustic Wedding*, are both in the very middle of these canvases, but do not at first catch the eye. So, because Satan is fallen, he is absurd and obscene; because he is destined to be overthrown, he is all but helpless now. And there he sits, right in the center of the picture of Mad Maggie: grotesquely thin and grotesquely tall, hunched on the top of his palace, with his back turned to the spectator (and the battle), his head sunk beneath a glass bubble enclosing the Ship of Fools, which symbolizes all earthly folly (Detail 4), and from his other end, which is

46

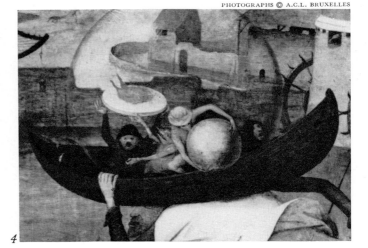

not a body but a broken eggshell, voiding a stream of money, useless and excremental.

It is a mad painting. Some people will not look at it after the first glance. It is almost incomprehensible. We do not even know its title: the Flemish art historian calls it *Dulle Griet*, but he may have made up the name himself instead of receiving it from tradition. Early descriptions of it are vague and show that it was an enigma soon after it was painted. One catalogue of 1648 may call it "A picture with a conflagration, in which is the Fury with miscellaneous monsters." The art historian Van Mander is more explicit, but says no more than this: "Mad Maggie is carrying off loot in front of hell: she is very crazy and wears an odd freakish get-up." One thing we do know, however. We know what her name means. Griet, which is short for Margaret in Flemish, was used especially for an ill-tempered, foul-mouthed, overbearing woman. So was Margot in French, and Meg in Scots and Irish: there is still a great cannon in Edinburgh Castle called Mucklemouthed Meg, Margaret with the Big Mouth. On the strength of this, we might guess that Bruegel himself gave the picture no such superficial title, but that it was coined by the public which saw a woman with a sword and armor, therefore a tough virago, with a wild look and surrounded by symbols of madness, therefore mad: Mad Meg or Mad Maggie.

One other thing we can tell when we study the picture. It shows a battle: on one side are the devils, and on the other the strong-minded women of the world which Bruegel knew. The women are winning, for they have routed or overthrown the infernal army and have started to carry off the loot of hell. Now, an obvious explanation would be that a foul-tempered woman is tough enough to intimidate the worst fiend, so the picture would be a very elaborate way of putting into visual symbolism some of the ill-natured medieval proverbs about bitter, gibing, railing wives. Even in Scripture (Proverbs 21:9) we read, "*It is* better to dwell in a corner of the housetop, than with a brawling woman in a wide house." But this is not quite satisfactory. The women are not brawling with their husbands. They are showing a wholesome energy in carrying out an admirable, almost saintly, aim: they have (at least temporarily) conquered hell

and humiliated the devils who tried to defend it. They do not even look savage and perverted, but rather, strong, positive, determined. It is both funny and encouraging to see their stout muscular arms thrashing the wriggling fiends and tying them up helplessly.

Another suggestion (made by a Belgian scholar, L. Jacobs-Havenith, writing in the *Revue Catholique des Idées et des Faits* for May, 1936) is that Griet and her comrades represent the spirit of War, which is worse than hell: War, which unlooses all contradictions, all passions. This might well be true— except that we normally think of War as hateful, while Griet and her friends are decent people doing something good.

Is there any solution, then? One other at least is possible. Perhaps the central figure is not a mad woman or a bad woman, but a good, heroic woman; more obviously, the other women are heroines also. I suggest therefore that the picture symbolizes the nobility and courage of the women of the Low Countries, whom Bruegel saw resisting so much cruelty and oppression almost all through his lifetime. I suggest that the central figure—a simple working-class woman who has been provoked once too often, has gone down to hell, led an army of her fellows to conquer it, and returned safely—represents the plain central virtues of ordinary wives and mothers, who, when enraged, will outface the devil himself. There have been other heroic female figures. Think of the Winged Victory; of the Greek evocations of Athena, the austere virgin with crested helmet and Gorgoned shield; of Rude's figure of the Marseillaise, shouting her song of victory from the Arc de Triomphe. But Bruegel, although he lived in the sixteenth century, was a man of the Middle Ages: his symbols were either medieval or drawn from the world he saw around him, its proverbs and its jokes, its superstitions and its human characteristics. And so, instead of a Winged Victory or an immortal goddess, he showed the dauntless courage of womanhood in the figure of an average housewife who has put on helmet and cuirass and sword for one special effort, but still, because she is coming back to live and work in this world, wears her plain black stockings, her apron, and her kitchen knife swinging at her side.

OVERLEAF: Bruegel's DULLE GRIET

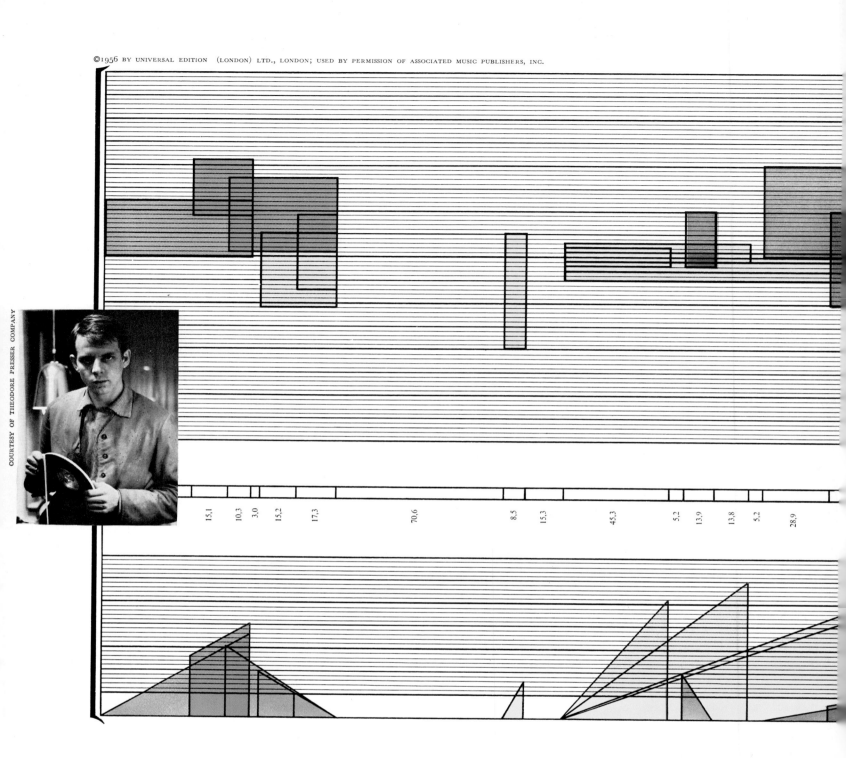

COURTESY OF THEODORE PRESSER COMPANY

15,1 10,3 3,0 15,2 17,3 70,6 8,5 15,3 45,3 5,2 13,9 13,8 5,2 28,9

A NEW MUSIC MADE WITH

What would Beethoven have done, had he possessed a tape recorder? He

sounds by "manipulating" old ones and adding electronic blips. This is

By DAVID RANDOLPH

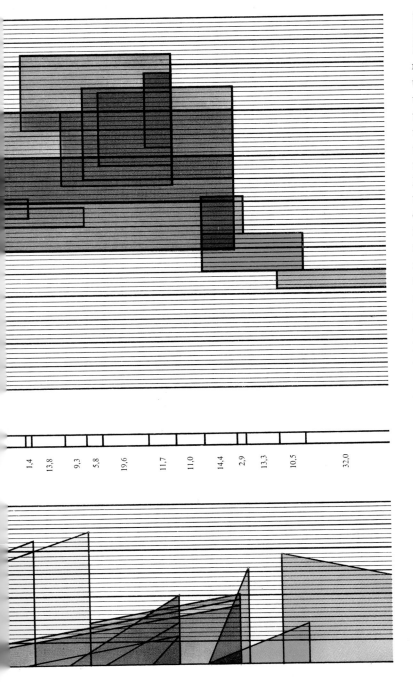

How many of those present in the auditorium of New York's Museum of Modern Art on October 28, 1952, realized that they were witnessing the beginning of a new era in the annals of music in America? As is the case with so many other important happenings—events that are later invested with a certain aura by the passage of time—this was announced with no special fanfare. In fact, the circumstances were becoming less and less dramatic as the evening progressed. The occasion was a concert of contemporary American music, conducted by Leopold Stokowski. The opening work had involved a small orchestra with piano; the next composition enlisted the services of only a quartet of wood-wind players. When they had finished, all the instruments, chairs, and music stands were removed; and a large speaker mounted in a cabinet, such as might be found in a high-quality phonograph, was placed in the center of the bare stage. Mr. Stokowski spoke briefly about the fact that the audience was now going to hear music conveyed directly from the composer to the listener, without the necessity of musicians to "interpret" it. Then he, too, left the stage, and the audience was left face to face with the speaker.

The first sound to emerge from the machine was a low rumble, suggesting the sound of the very lowest notes on the piano. That was followed by what was obviously a piano, but within the first few moments it became apparent that this was not just an ordinary recording of a piano. A chord was struck, but no sooner had the sound begun than it was immediately cut off in a manner that could never be achieved by any pianist. For the next seven minutes the audience listened to a composition made possible by electronic manipulation of the sounds of the piano, joined at a few spots by the sounds of human voices. With this hearing (I hesitate to use the word *performance*) of Vladimir Ussachevsky's *Sonic Contours*, tape recorder music had made

This diagram represents music as the young German composer Karlheinz Stockhausen (left) writes it, in a departure as startling to the ear as its score is to the eye. Using no conventional instruments, Stockhausen composes sounds by means of electronic oscillators and then tapes the results. In the above (from his Electronic Study II*) the upper graph indicates the pitch and duration of his sounds on a rising scale of frequencies, corresponding to the notes a "conventional" composer would write on staves. Mixtures and overlappings of sounds are indicated in the original score by shadings of increasing thickness to denote density; here, to help show their variety, they are indicated by progressions of color. The lower diagram, proceeding simultaneously with the upper, specifies the volume or intensity of the sounds on a scale of decibels, as an earlier composer might set down crescendo or diminuendo marks above his notes. Between them runs a time band giving the rate at which the work is to be "realized," written in terms of centimeter lengths of tape running at a fixed speed. Here automation takes over: the performer of a conventional work is of course free to pick his own tempi, within the limits of the composer's instructions to play lento, allegretto, or presto, etc.*

A MACHINE

might have created wholly new

what insurgents are doing now

its official bow in the United States.

The concept of *musique concrète*, as it is called by the French, or "tapesichord" music, as it is sometimes referred to on this side of the ocean, has been making more and more of a stir in the world of music. It has attracted the support of such figures as Stokowski, Alfred Wallenstein, and Hermann Scherchen. It has made its impact felt in the movies and television. In the field of popular song, it has assaulted the ears of countless millions in "Purple People Eater" —the People Eater's toy horn being a saxophone recorded on tape at low speed and then played back at very high speed.

What is it? How is it achieved, and what is it likely to do to our concept of music?

Briefly, it is music produced with the aid of electronics; it has been made possible through the invention of the tape recorder.

Despite the fact that the subject seems to be bristling with technical terminology comprehensible only to a trained engineer, there is nothing about its basic principles that cannot be understood by the layman.

Simply put, the tape recorder has given the composer a means of *manipulating* sound in ways that were previously out of the question. To be sure, composers throughout history can be said to have done nothing more than to "manipulate" sounds, but even the most advanced composition played by any number or any combination of instruments cannot produce the kinds of sounds that the tape recorder makes possible. In a live performance, all sounds immediately disappear. As sad as it may seem to realize that in any actual performance of a musical work, the music "dies as soon as it is born," this is a very fortunate thing: if sounds did not disappear, but remained around for long periods of time, music as we know it would be impossible.

Nevertheless, if sounds could be captured and preserved in some tangible form that would allow them to be "handled," the composer's materials would be enlarged. An obvious answer would be the phonograph disc that has been available for well over half a century. But think for a moment of the nature of the phonograph record—either the modern, long-playing, microgroove disc, or its predecessor, the 78 rpm record. Both are based on the same principle: the sounds are preserved in a spiral groove that is engraved on a rigid surface. Granted this is a most ingenious means of recording a musical work; but notice how poorly it lends itself to the isolation of any minute portion of the work and above all, to the *manipulation* of those minute portions.

Now, suppose for a moment that it were possible to "unwind" the spiral grooves on a disc, so that, instead of their being rigidly fixed and therefore inaccessible, they were now in one long line, like a long piece of thread. The entire thing could then be wound on a spool, and any one section could be isolated from the others and "handled" at will. This, in essence, is the nature of a tape recording. The tape, however, is a thin, flat ribbon, a quarter of an inch wide.

BILL AND GWEN SLOAN

ROLLIE MCKENNA

Left, a Stockhausen electronic composition is produced without performers in the studio of the West German radio station at Cologne. Right, the scientist, composer, and musician Pièrre Schaeffer, leader of the Paris musique concrète group, stands amid electronic equipment. Below left, Edgard Varèse, pioneer rebel against what he terms "the tyranny of the tempered scale," sits at the New York desk at which he has manipulated "natural" sounds to create such taped works as Deserts *and* Poème Electronique, *the latter played daily to mass audiences at last year's Brussels Fair. Below right, Igor Stravinsky examines a score shown him by Pierre Boulez, another member of the* musique concrète *group and often called the* enfant terrible *of comtemporary music. At bottom, two Columbia University music professors, Otto Luening and Vladimir Ussachevsky, collaborate on experiments in modifying the sounds of musical instruments by electronic means. The performance of several of their compositions, at a concert at the Museum of Modern Art in 1952 under Leopold Stokowski's direction, introduced the realm of "tapesichord" music to America.*

The important point to notice is that any one phrase, or, for that matter, any one single sound can now be located precisely, and, because it is preserved on a piece of ribbon that can be held in the hand, it lends itself to all manner of manipulation. Suppose, for a moment, that we have recorded on the ribbon the sound of a single note that was played originally on the piano. It is characteristic of the sound of the piano to start with the percussive effect of the hammer striking the string. The tone, or the note itself, then follows, and it dies away quite rapidly. It is because of these two characteristics, among others, that we recognize the sound of the piano and can distinguish it from that of other instruments. Now let us locate on the tape just the spot at which the percussive knock of the hammer is recorded, and, using a pair of scissors, cut it out and splice the tape together again, using a piece of cellophane tape. When we play that tape, we now have a sound that stemmed from the piano, but that could not be produced by a "live" pianist. This is what is meant when we say that the tape recorder has given the composer a means of manipulating or handling sounds in ways that could have been only imagined before.

Now, you might give free rein to your own imagination and think of the various ways in which sounds can be handled on the tape. Cut away the tone and preserve the part with the knock of the piano's hammer, and you have the very thing that the audience heard near the beginning of Ussachevsky's *Sonic Contours.* A certain emotional effect results from this sudden stopping of the piano tone. Play the tape backward (something that cannot be done conveniently with a phonograph disc but is a simple matter with tape) and you have the unusual effect of the piano sound starting as if from nowhere and suddenly *ending* with the percussive knock! Record a fairly low note and play it back at very slow speed, and the result is a note far lower than any that can be achieved on the piano. Playing the tape at a much faster speed raises the pitch and also causes notes to be played far more rapidly than could be done with human hands. It is a simple matter with a tape recorder to add what sounds like an echo, thus increasing the range of effects.

If these and many other techniques are extended to all the other instruments, the range of possible effects becomes enormous. Flutes can be made to growl in unaccustomed depths. Percussion instruments can be the source of endless delights—and the human voice can produce results that stagger the imagination!

All of this stems from conventional musical instruments, whose sounds are manipulated on tape. This is the basis of one of the three main schools of electronic music. Its outstanding practitioners in this country are two soft-spoken Columbia University music professors, Vladimir Ussachevsky and Otto Luening.

Ussachevsky, born in Manchuria, came to the United States in 1930 with the intention of becoming an engineer. Talked out of the idea by several depression-hit professionals, he turned his attention to music and completed his graduate studies at the Eastman School of Music, where several of his works were performed. His experiments in composing music with the tape recorder began in 1951, and the next year he began collaborating with American-born Otto Luening, who had studied music in Munich and Zurich, and privately with Busoni. The catalogue of Luening's compositions for conventional instruments runs to several pages of small type, and in the electronics field you can now hear in your own home on an LP record his *Fantasy in Space*, *Invention*, and *Low Speed*. The two composers are also now represented on discs by their joint electronic creations, *A Poem in Cycles and Bells*, *Suite from King Lear*, and *Rhapsodic Variations for Tape Recorder and Orchestra*.

But thanks to the versatility of the tape recorder, composers are now able to go beyond conventional instruments and extend their sources of sounds into new realms. Why not use the sounds of nature: birds, ocean breakers, human heartbeats, railroads, the hum of an insect, laughter, drops of water, footsteps, human speech, and the like? Captured on tape and subjected to electronic manipulation, these sounds can also be the basis for music. The transformations can make the original sources unrecognizable—or, if the composer wishes, he can retain some of their original characteristics. This use of natural or "concrete" sounds is the basis of the second of the schools of composition for tape recorder. It was developed by the *Groupe de Recherches de Musique Concrète* in Paris, the chief exponents of which are Pierre Schaeffer and Pierre Henry.

It is Pierre Schaeffer who must be credited with the first composition of this kind. This versatile young man—a traveler, author of novels and travel stories, engineer, and amateur musician—was working in the Research Department of the French Radio in 1948, when it occurred to him that sounds might be manipulated after they had been captured on tape. In October of that year there was broadcast over the French Radio his *Etude aux Chemins de Fer*, based on the sounds of railroad trains. One year later the name *musique concrète* came into being. As Schaeffer himself explains, it was meant "to describe this new way of making music which allows the composer to work from the start with his actual sound materials, directly, as a painter works with pigments and canvas; a sculptor with clay or stone."

There has already been considerable intermixing of these two electronic approaches—one from conventional instruments and the other from sounds in nature. The distinguishing characteristics of the two are by no means rigidly adhered to by composers of the contrasting schools. But there is also a third school in which little such freedom is permitted. In this approach, which originated in Germany, almost the only sounds used are produced mechanically—that is, in an electronic machine itself. Most of us are familiar with the phenomenon by which our bodies can cause a defective radio or TV unit to emit strange sounds. This principle, much refined, is the basis of the sounds used by the German school. They are produced by oscillators within the electronic system itself. Their howls, squeals, and growls can be very carefully controlled. Originating thus, the "music" is devoid of any associations that might be brought to mind by the sounds of conventional musical instruments. The center of this radical school is Cologne, and its chief representative is Karlheinz Stockhausen, a young man who was associated with the *musique concrète* group while studying with Olivier Messiaen in Paris, and who today is retained by the West German Radio as staff composer. Young Stockhausen, sitting down with his electronic dials and circuits, "composes" from them on tapes combinations and sequences that have no precedent anywhere.

Now what about the place of this new tape recorder music as a whole? Is it aesthetically valid? What is it likely to do to our listening habits? How will it affect the concert world? Is the practicing musician about to be replaced, and will our music-making become dehumanized as a result of the introduction of this mechanical element?

I think we must grant that, theoretically, music created with the tape recorder is as valid as is a Bach fugue or a Beethoven symphony. In the final analysis, all these works are organizations of sound. What is a melody but a succession of sounds organized according to certain principles? And what is a fugue but the further organization of several melodies, along lines that seem amazingly similar to those

CONTINUED ON PAGE 124

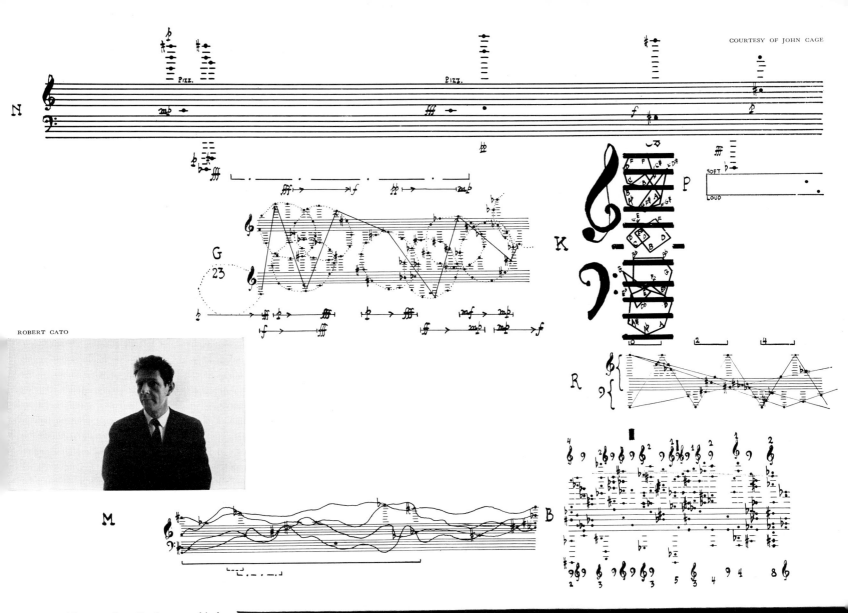

ROBERT CATO

New music calls for new kinds of notation. The American John Cage (above) composes not only for tape but for what he calls the "prepared piano," inserting screws and wood blocks among its strings to produce unprecedented sounds for his trance-like improvisations, never the same twice. This calligraphic shorthand (from his Concerto for Piano and Orchestra) suggests his audacity. Far soberer, visually, is this diagram page of an early Ussachevsky-Luening electronic work—a "mixing score" for three tracks of prepared sound on magnetic tape.

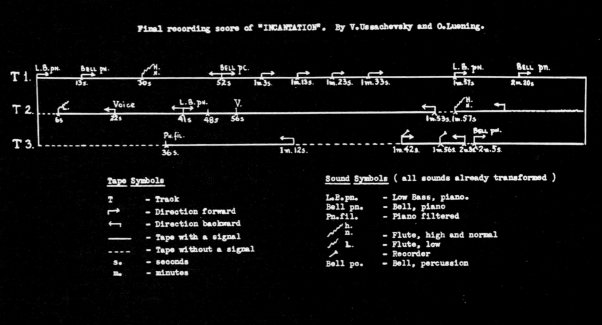

Final recording score of "INCANTATION". By V. Ussachevsky and O. Luening.

Tape Symbols

T — Track
→ — Direction forward
← — Direction backward
— — Tape with a signal
---- — Tape without a signal
S. — seconds
m. — minutes

Sound Symbols (all sounds already transformed)

L.B.pn. — Low Bass, piano.
Bell pn. — Bell, piano
Pn.fil. — Piano filtered
h. n. — Flute, high and normal
l. — Flute, low
— Recorder
Bell pc. — Bell, percussion

MY WORLD
and what happened to it

Where are the spats, the butlers, the under butlers, the gay and innocuous young

scions of the favorite few? Gone, says their chronicler—but not quite. And not forgotten

By P. G. WODEHOUSE

It was always a small world—one of the smallest I ever met, as Bertie Wooster would say. In London it was bounded on the east by St. James Street, on the west by Hyde Park Corner, by Oxford Street on the north, and by Piccadilly on the south, overflowing in the rural districts to country houses in Shropshire and other delectable counties. And now it is not even small, it is nonexistent.

This is pointed out to me every time a new book of mine dealing with Jeeves or Blandings Castle or the Drones Club is published in England. "Edwardian!" the critics hiss at me. (It is not easy to hiss the word *Edwardian*, containing, as it does, no sibilant, but they manage it.) And I shuffle my feet and say, "Yes, I suppose you're right." After all, I tell myself, there has been no generic term for the type of young man who figures in my stories, since he used to be called a knut in the pre-First-War days, which certainly seems to suggest that the species has died out like the macaronis of the Regency and the whiskered mashers of the Victorian age.

But sometimes I am in a more defiant mood. Mine, I protest, are historical novels. Nobody objects when an author writes the sort of things that begin, "More skilled though I am at wielding the broadsword than the quill, I will set down for all to read the tale of how I, plain John Blunt, did follow my dear liege to the wars when Harry, y-clept the fifth, sat on our English throne." Then why am I not to be allowed to set down for all to read the tale of how the Hon. J. Blunt got fined five pounds by the magistrate at Bosher Street Police Court for disorderly conduct on Boat Race Night? Unfair discrimination is the phrase that springs to the lips.

I suppose one thing that makes these drones of mine seem creatures of a dead past is that with the exception of Oofy Prosser, the club millionaire, they are genial and good-tempered, friends of all the world. In these days when everybody hates everybody else, anyone who is not snarling at something—or at everything—is an anachronism. The Edwardian knut was never an angry young man. He would get a little cross, perhaps, if his man Meadows sent him out some morning with odd spats on, but his normal outlook on life was sunny. He was a humble, kindly soul, who knew he was a silly ass but hoped you wouldn't mind. Portrayed on the stage by George Grossmith and G. P. Huntley, he was a lovable figure, warming the hearts of all. You might disapprove of him for not being a world's worker, but you could not help being fond of him.

Though, as a matter of fact, many of the members of my Drones Club *are* world's workers. Freddie Threepwood is a vice-president at Donaldson's Dog-Joy, Inc., of Long Island City, and sells as smart a dog biscuit as the best of them. Bingo Little edits *Wee Tots*, the popular journal for the

The Wodehouse world is well portrayed by Brockbank in this Punch *cartoon of 1951. Here we see a noble, gouty lord and his coroneted lady entertaining the vicar at tea with the usual supporting cast: butler, maid, bagpiper, guardsman, chimney sweep, and a hunt in full cry. The young master in Eton garb rolls his hoop in the path of his grouse-shooting sister. War has intruded only slightly, in a Battle of Britain box score on one pillar and a remembrance from Adolf Hitler at lower left, happily converted to a flower holder. This cartoon was presented by* Punch *as the Americans' "Mistaken View of the British." Certainly the American view of England between the wars owed a good deal to Mr. Wodehouse's novels.*

nursery and the home; Catsmeat Potter-Pirbright has played the juvenile in a number of West End drawing-room comedies, generally coming on early in Act One with a cheery "Tennis, anyone?"; and even Bertie Wooster once wrote an article for his Aunt Dahlia's weekly, *Milady's Boudoir*, on "What the Well-Dressed Man Is Wearing." Your drone can always work if he feels like it. It is very seldom, of course, that he does feel like it. He prefers just to exist beautifully.

Two things caused the decline of the drone, or knut, the first of which was that hard times hit younger sons. Most knuts were younger sons, and in the reign of good King Edward the position of the younger son in aristocratic families was . . . what's the word, Jeeves? Anomalous? You're sure? Right ho, anomalous. Thank you, Jeeves. Putting it another way, he was a trifle on the superfluous side, his standing about that of the litter of kittens which the household cat deposits in the drawer where you keep your clean shirts.

What generally happened was this. An Earl, let us say, begat an heir. So far, so good. One can always do with an heir. But then—these earls never know when to stop—he begat—absent-mindedly, as it were—a second son and this time was not any too pleased about the state of affairs. Unlike the male codfish which, becoming the father of three million five hundred thousand little codfish, cheerfully resolves to love them all, the aristocrat of those days found the younger son definitely a nuisance. Unless he went into the Church and became a curate—which as a rule he stoutly declined to do—it was difficult to see how to fit him in. But there he was, requiring his calories just the same as if he had been the first in succession. It made the Earl feel that he was up against something hard to handle.

"Can't let Algy starve," he said to himself, and forked out a monthly allowance. And so there came into being a group of ornamental young men whom the ravens fed. Like the lilies of the field, they toiled not, neither did they spin, but lived quite contentedly on the paternal dole. Their wants were few. Provided they could secure the services of a tailor who was prepared to accept charm of manner as a substitute for hard cash—and it was extraordinary

WALLACE MORGAN

how full London was of altruistic tailors in the early nineteen hundreds—they asked for little more. In short, so long as the ravens continued to do their stuff, they were in that blissful condition known as sitting pretty. Then the economic factor reared its ugly head. There were global wars, and if you have global wars you cannot have happy well-fed younger sons. Income tax and supertax shot up like rocketing pheasants, and the Earl found himself doing some constructive thinking. A bright idea occurred to him, and the more he turned it over in his mind, the better he liked it.

"Dash it all," he said to his Countess as they sat one night trying to balance the budget, "*Why* can't I?"

"Why can't you what?" said she.

"Let Algy starve."

"Algy who?"

"Our Algy."

"You mean our second son, the Hon. Algernon Blair Trefusis ffinch-ffinch?"

"That's right. He's getting into my ribs to the tune of a cool thousand quid a year because I felt I couldn't let him starve. The point I'm making is, why *not* let the young blighter starve?"

"It's a thought," the Countess agreed. "Yes, a very sound scheme. We all eat too much these days, anyway."

So the ravens were retired from active duty, and Algy, faced with the prospect of not getting his three square meals a day unless he worked for them, hurried out and found a job, with the result that as of even date any poor hack like myself who, wishing to turn an honest penny, writes stories about him and all the other Algys, Freddies, Claudes, and Berties, automatically becomes Edwardian.

The second thing that led to the elimination of the knut was the passing of the spat. In the brave old days spats were the hallmark of the young-feller-me-lad-about-town, the foundation stone on which his whole policy was based, and it is sad to reflect that a generation has arisen that does not know what spats were. I once wrote a book called *Young Men In Spats*. I could not use that title today.

Spatterdashes was, I believe, their full name, and they were made of white cloth and buttoned around the ankles, partly no doubt to prevent the socks from getting dashed with spatter but principally because they lent a sort of gay diablerie to the wearer's appearance. The monocle might or might not be worn, according to taste, but spats, like the tightly rolled umbrella, were obligatory.

I was never myself by knut standards really dressy as a young man (*circa* 1905), for a certain anemia of the exchequer compelled me to go about my social duties in my brother's castoff frock coat and trousers, neither of which fitted me, and a top hat bequeathed to me by an uncle with a head some sizes larger than mine, but my umbrella was always rolled as tight as a drum, and though spats cost money I had mine all right. There they were, bright and gleaming, fascinating the passers-by and causing seedy strangers who hoped for largesse to address me as "Captain" or sometimes even as "M'lord." Many a butler, opening the front door to me and wincing visibly at the sight of my topper, would lower his eyes, see the spats, and give a little sigh of relief, as much as to say, "Not quite what we are accustomed to at the northern end, perhaps, but unexceptionable to the south."

Naturally, if you cut off a fellow's allowance, he cannot afford spats, and without spats he is a spent force. Deprived of these indispensable adjuncts, the knut threw in the towel and called it a day. And just as the spat has vanished and the knut has vanished, so has the country house, in the deepest and fullest sense of the term, also ceased to exist. And it was into the country houses, if you remember, that my little world overflowed.

Mark you, the stately homes of England, of which Felicia Hemans thought so highly, still stand as beautiful as ever amidst their tall ancestral trees o'er all the pleasant land,* and if you have half a crown (thirty-five cents at the present rate of exchange) you can go and ramble over them. Drop in, for instance, on the Duke of Bedford at Woburn Abbey with your half-crown in your hot little hand, and you will not only be greeted by His Grace in person and shown the house and all its artistic treasures but will get a snack lunch and be able to listen to the latest song hits on the jukebox. The same conditions prevail at Chatsworth, the Duke of Devonshire's little place up Derbyshire way, and in some three hundred other stately homes now in the side-show business.

But the country house as one used to know it in the old days, with its careless hospitality and grace of living, is a thing of the past. The trouble with all these Abbeys and Halls and Towers or whatever they called themselves was that the early ancestors who built them had such spacious ideas. Home, they considered, was not home unless you had accommodation for fifty guests and a few hundred varlets and scurvy knaves, and in recent times the supply of scurvy knaves and varlets has given out.

*See the article by J. H. Plumb, "The Noble Houses of Eighteenth-Century England," in HORIZON, November, 1958.

WIDE WORLD PHOTOS

One of the few survivals of the Wodehouse era is the young Duke of Kent, cousin of the Queen. A lover of all-night rock-'n'-roll parties, he has delighted the London press by such high jinks as sprinkling passers-by with champagne and watching fellow guests get dunked in the Thames. "He is always behaving," says Mr. Wodehouse, fondly, "like someone out of my novels."

Just before the First World War, I was working on a novel dealing with life at a large country house—Blanding's Castle, in case you missed the book, the Shropshire seat of Clarence, ninth Earl of Emsworth—and it was essential for me to inform myself about the personnel of the Servant's Hall at a place like that, my hero (from the best motives) having taken on the duties of a visiting valet. I knew a man who knew a lot of dukes and earls, and I asked him to give me the facts. They were as follows:

Take, my friend said, the Duke of Portland. Being a duke is sort of tough. It is not a thing you can make a success of singlehanded. You need helpers. Here is the list of the Duke of Portland's co-workers:

Chief Steward or Major Domo	Kitchen porter
Steward	Six odd men
Wine butler	Head housekeeper
Under butler	Valets
Groom of the Chambers	Lady's maids
Four footmen	Head coachman
Steward's Room footmen	Second coachman
Master of Servant's Hall	Ten grooms
Two page boys	Twenty strappers
Head chef	Head chauffeur
Second chef	Fifteen chauffeurs
Head baker	Six house gardeners
Second baker	Forty gardeners
Head kitchen maid	Fifty roadmen
Two under kitchen maids	Head laundress
Vegetable maid	Twelve laundresses
Three scullery maids	Head window cleaner
Head stillroom maid	Five window cleaners
Three stillroom maids	Six engineers
Hall porter	Four firemen
Two hall boys	Three night watchmen

With the assistance of these, working shoulder to shoulder like the Boys of the Old Brigade, His Grace of Portland managed to get by all right and was as happy a duke as you could wish. The only thing that bothered him was that he disliked ringing a bell when he wanted anything, and this might have embittered his life, had he not got the idea of having a footman always within earshot behind a screen, ready to spring forward when he shouted "Hi!" which was

CONTINUED ON PAGE 127

A LOST CIVILIZATION IN THE CAMBODIAN JUNGLE TELLS

ITS STORY IN FABLED TEMPLES AND SCULPTURES MADE BY

NAMELESS ARTISTS IN THE SERVICE OF DEMIGOD KINGS

ANGKOR

By SANTHA RAMA RAU

Three or four centuries ago, according to the story you are certain to hear in Cambodia, a missionary was walking from the small Cambodian town of Siemréap through the tangled jungle that surrounds it to a village deep in the forests. On his way along one of the narrow jungle paths, he tripped on a stone half-hidden by the crawling vines and underbrush of the tropical jungle. He stopped to look more carefully at the rock, a dark gray, unusual in Cambodia, and what he saw made him scrape away some of the leaves and lichen and examine the rock more closely still. It was carved. It had obviously been shaped by an expert craftsman. Evidently it represented some figure of enormous authority—that much was clear from the incontrovertible power of the sculpture. A deity, perhaps, or a long-forgotten king. The missionary reported his find to other members of his order when he returned from his journey.

From that point the story of the discovery of the magnificent ruins of Angkor, that extraordinary, evocative, mysterious, and compelling capital of a vanished empire, changes according to whether you hear it from foreigners or from the Cambodians. One version tells you that the missionaries wanted to follow up their first mysterious clue to the historical wealth hidden in the Cambodian jungle, but they had neither the money nor the leisure to conduct large-scale archaeological work. Other authorities, even years later, were not particularly interested in what must have sounded like a most improbable fantasy; while the Cambodians, who knew of the tree-strangled, partly buried treasure of their jungles, viewed the ruins with a kind of superstitious horror. To them it was a ghost town of a sort, haunted by unpredictable spirits. A Frenchman, the *conseiller* of the district before Cambodian independence, once remarked, "If you ask one of the natives here who built these incredible ruins they will tell you, 'They were built by the gods.'"

The other version is that the missionaries, alarmed by the thought that their unexpected discovery might revitalize an old religion or give added strength to the present Buddhism, prudently kept quiet about the great ruined buildings, monuments, and temples in the heart of Cambodia. Surely these stone deities, these great uncompromising faces, could only attract the Cambodians back to idolatry. Better leave it all alone.

In any case, this much is true: the actual excavations and

ART AND NATURE IN MORTAL COMBAT:

A twelfth-century image on a wall at Angkor contends with encroaching banyan vines and fig trees. Of this jungle battle, historian Arnold Toynbee wrote after a visit, "Look at that gigantic tree which has leapt, like a panther, on to this unhappy building's back and is tearing its victim to pieces with its cruel claws. That tree is a veritable carnivore in slow motion. Keep it continuously exposed to the lens of a film camera for a hundred years, and then speed up the apparatus till you can display a century's action in one minute. You will see this panther-tree leaping swiftly and savagely to its kill. And now look at this outer gateway of a temple enclosure. A seedling has planted itself on the crown of the gatehouse roof and has swollen into a boa constrictor with as many bodies as a Hindu god has arms and legs. . . . "

reconstruction of Angkor did not begin until 1907, when French experts, archaeologists, and historians set to work to explore and restore one of the greatest groups of ruins in the world and to uncover the history of one of its shortest, most glorious, and most destructive empires. The Khmers, the people of central Cambodia, whose ancient capital was Angkor, recorded their rise and fall over five centuries— their conquests, achievements, their prides and sorrows, their religion, and their pleasures—all in stone. To an enthralling extent, Angkor is a sculptured book of history and legend intertwined.

Before the great Angkorean period that began in about A.D. 800, virtually nothing is known about Cambodia's early life. There is a story that at one time the country was ruled by a queen with the pleasing name of "Willow Leaf." There was nothing but peace and contentment in her kingdom, and her people led idyllic lives. Also, they wore no clothes. Eventually, a Brahmin traveling from India came to visit Queen Willow Leaf, and although he was quite alarmed by the nakedness all around him, still he fell in love with the Queen. He gave her the first cloth that she had ever seen and persuaded her to wrap herself in it. This so delighted her that she married the Brahmin and together they founded the ruling line of Cambodia that was, at its most glorious moment, to include the Khmer kings.

A slightly more factual account of the conversion of the Cambodians to Hinduism comes from those ancient Chinese travelers who wandered all over Asia and somehow managed to keep up a voluminous correspondence with their people at home, describing the countries and cities that they visited. From them we get a picture of early Cambodians worshiping "the Spirits of Heaven" and representing them in images of stone. "Those with two faces have four arms, and those with four faces have eight arms." You can still see those Hindu deities in the early temples of the Angkor area.

Another Chinese document, of the fifth century, records the request of the Cambodian king for help from the Chinese emperor in repelling an enemy king. It is only from these disjointed bits of evidence that one can form some idea of the great waves of religious and cultural imperialism that reached Cambodia from India, and of the bitter wars that were fought on the southeast Asian mainland before Cambodia established its domination of all its neighbors.

Late in the seventh century a rebellion began in one of Cambodia's vassal states. It was to prove overwhelmingly successful, for it captured the whole country and established the Khmer dynasty as its rulers. It was not until more than a hundred years later that the first of the "constructor-kings" emerged—or, in the words of the old records, "rose like a fresh lotus." In the more than fifty years of Jayavarman II's reign, there began the sweeping conquests of the Khmers abroad, and the building of the fantastic city of Angkor Thom at home. In the centuries that followed, the Khmer armies (whose strength has been estimated as up to five million men) subdued most of the mainland of southeast Asia and extracted a nervous and conciliating tribute from places as remote as Malaya and the Indonesian Islands, and all the time the legends of the wonder and wealth of Angkor grew.

It is not surprising that a truly compelling kind of *folie de grandeur* began to grip the Khmer kings. They worshiped their gods in the temples they had built, but simultaneously they deified themselves. Their religion was changing from Hinduism to Buddhism as successive waves of priests and pilgrims came to Angkor, but the Khmers transmuted it into a Buddhism unlike any other form in the world. At the same time they kept a kind of overlay of Hinduism in the forms of their religion. When the uniquely beautiful temple of Bayon was built, it embodied this new mixture of ideas. From the fifty towers of Bayon, the royal temple in the heart of the royal enclosure of Angkor Thom, immense stone faces stare out over the forest and the other buildings. It is a design unknown in the parent culture of India.

In those features—the long, calm eyes, the mouth set just short of a smile, the expression of knowledge and authority—the long-ago Khmers and their subject peoples saw both the portrait of Lokesvara, the Compassionate Buddha, and equally, the face of their king in constant watchfulness over even the distant reaches of his empire. Yet they seemed to find no contradiction in the fact that the temple was also dedicated to Shiva. There is a curious fact to set against the supreme arrogance of the lives of the Khmer god-kings. There is no record of their deaths. Were they cremated, as Hindus? Or buried, as Buddhists? And if so, where? In the temples? In the forest? In some as yet undiscovered burial ground? Nobody knows. A strongly argued theory is that the same temples, built for the gods, were also intended to enshrine the dead bodies of the kings.

When you go to Angkor now, your first view of the ancient city will probably be of the temple of Angkor Vat. From the plane window you will see its vast rectangle scraped free from the jungle. From your hotel room you will see its gray towers rising above the trees. That first sight of Angkor Vat cannot fail to be impressive. Even if you do not agree with the French explorer Henri Mouhot that "this architectural work perhaps has not and perhaps never has had its equal on the face of the globe," still, the extraordinary scale, the incredible expenditure of talent and wealth on its decorations, carvings, buildings, will convince you that it is deservedly the most renowned monument of a city built for gods and kings. And all the time you are there you will be haunted by the thought that in the end the jungle was stronger than those dead Khmers whose magnificence was famous and powerful throughout Asia.

As you explore Angkor Vat in greater detail, you will find yourself entering that lost life of the Khmers with an almost chilling immediacy. It is there all around you, as soon as you cross the long stone bridge over the moat, pass the low wall enclosing the temple grounds, and enter the outer galleries. There, on acres of wall space around miles of galleries, are the celebrated bas-reliefs of Angkor, its greatest wonder and its most explicit record. Thousands upon thousands of brilliant craftsmen and artisans labored under the royal command to describe with unparalleled precision the life of the Khmers at their most glorious period. The climactic scenes from Hindu mythology, essential to their arts and religion, are spread in a great, turbulent panorama across these walls. The stories from the Hindu epics, the *Mahabharata* and the *Ramayana*, are illustrated in meticulous detail. The great armies with their battalions of cavalry, their brigades of foot soldiers, their elephants jeweled and decorated for fantastic wars, charge across the walls, pennants flying, lances ready, crossbows drawn. The vitality of these carvings is so intense that your first impulse can well be to step back, out of the way, before you remember that these battles are in stone and a thousand years old.

Then there are the quieter scenes—the lavishness of court life, the musicians, the dancers, the courtiers. Or the everyday activity of the royal city, the workers and craftsmen and traders. In nearby Bayon, with even more convincing reality, you can see the pedestrian, but wonderfully lively, scenes of the fishermen pulling out into the great lake near Angkor to bring in loads of fish for the city; or a baker with his assistants —one firing the oven, some bringing in loaves ready to be baked, others carrying away the ones that are done; or a woman washing her hair or taking care of her children and playing games with them. You can see lines of coolies, with loads slung on bamboo poles across their shoulders, trotting down the streets—you can see them still, in real life, on any road in Cambodia. Or the peasants and farmers, using the same kind of plows depicted in the Angkor reliefs, the oxen pulling the same sort of carts with their giant wheels, or the forests and jungles of Cambodia, the animals and the hunters. And always present, in everything, are the gods and the demons and the mythological kings—an evocation of a life, an age, a whole world. From the outer galleries you move into the courtyards they enclose, for Angkor Vat is built on the conventional Hindu plan of diminishing rectangles fitted within each other like a series of Chinese boxes. In each courtyard are the crumbling remnants of the buildings that were necessary to this great complex of religion and royalty —the libraries, the halls of meditation, the special shrines, the minor temples, and always the dance pavilions where the palace dancers and the temple dancers used to perform.

You see them everywhere in Angkor. Those dancers are carved on hundreds of pillars and lintels; they catch your eye a dozen times as you walk down a corridor; from the shadows of a niche or a dark corner they hold their moment of arrested life. On outer walls they are chiseled out sharply by sunlight and shade. They are among the most elegant women in the world, draped in a wisp of diaphanous cloth, with impossibly tiny waists and full, round breasts like pomegranates; their hair is dressed in elaborate loops and knots, wound with pearls and flowers; their wrists and necks are encrusted with jewelry; their fingers curl backwards like the petals of a tiger lily, and the traditionally enigmatic half-smile of the dancer is always on their lips. Their magic is infallible, both to visitors and to Cambodians. A modern Cambodian poet wrote of their sculptured allure, "The eye does not tire, the soul is delighted, the heart is never satisfied. One cannot make up one's mind to leave them. They are no longer figures made by human hands; they are living women, beautiful and gracious."

Once I saw the present palace dancers of the king of Cambodia perform on one of the dance platforms of Angkor

Vat. It was an extraordinary, almost a ghostly experience because all at once, when the dancers began their infinitely graceful, highly stylized re-enactments of the old Hindu stories, when the rippling, liquid music of the Cambodian orchestra started, and the ivory horns were raised, the bamboo xylophones and the drums were struck, a sudden life came to the dead world of Angkor. There, lit by flickering palm leaf torches, were the dancers from the carvings, with the same tapering, curving fingers fluttering like birds, the same jeweled extravagance of dress, the same ornate headdresses, the same secret dancer's smile. All around in the darkness the Cambodian people, the descendants of the Khmers, watched with enormous eyes the fragments of their heritage brought to a glittering reality.

At the heart of Angkor Vat is what remains of the most sacred of the shrines, a steep, heavily carved pyramid of stone holding the holy chambers that were penetrated only by the priests and the kings. Now, if you have a good head for heights, you can climb the narrow, dizzying steps to those dark cells and coldly austere passages. They did not always contain only this emptiness and the musty smell of bats. At one time, according to the historians, the richest of Angkor's treasures were set against these polished stone walls. Here the images and symbols of the Brahminic and later the Buddhist deities were coated with gold, studded with precious stones—all of it looted long ago, leaving these narrow unadorned caves.

From this height, when you turn to look out between the pillars of a gallery at the royal view of the temple, you see the whole of Angkor Vat stretched below you like an architect's model. At once you grasp the nobility of the design that can blend the immense scale of the galleries and court-

TEXT CONTINUED ON PAGE 81

A portfolio of photographs begins overleaf

THE MYSTERIOUS SPLENDORS OF ANGKOR

*A Portfolio
of Photographs by*
ERNST HAAS

The air route is the best for approaching rediscovered Angkor, deep in the north-west Cambodian jungles that surround it and that long submerged it. Recently the noted Austrian photographer Ernst Haas took in his equipment by this means to record its vast remains. The following sixteen pages present his color photographs.

In the picture above, the visitor by air is looking down upon the temple of Angkor Vat, built in the early twelfth century by King Suryavarman II to the glory of the Hindu god Vishnu. About a mile to the north lies the royal walled city of Angkor Thom, with its five huge gates and its fifty towers of Bayon—seat of a dynasty that rose to imperial splendor only to vanish without any traces beyond these in stone.

Built of rubbed and perfectly fitted blocks of laterite faced with sandstone, without use of mortar, many structures resisted nature's strangulation. Others sprang apart when iron binding clamps decayed or were looted. In our own era, French archae-ologists cleared the jungle and meticulously restored fallen blocks to their original places, using new materials only when a stone was entirely missing. Thereby one of the world's great monuments was literally brought back to light.

At the time of Angkor's glory, the influence of Buddhism, transported from India shortly after Hinduism, had also become great in Indochina. Many shrines were dedicated to "bodhisattvas," or future buddhas. Khmer kings often had them-selves represented in such form, indicating that through their kindness and munifi-cence they had achieved sainthood. The sandstone head that opens the portfolio portrays some sainted individual in the form of Lokesvara—a popular bodhisattva who helped men achieve ultimate release from worldly pains in the complete spiritual reward of the state of nirvana.

The head was found outside the walls of Angkor Thom in the ruined city of Preah Khan. Now wholly overgrown, Preah Khan was proclaimed to be holier even than Allahabad in India, and the waters that surround it were thought to cleanse mud from the soul.

"A rival to that of Solomon, erected by some ancient Michelangelo . . . it is grander than anything left to us by Greece and Rome," wrote the first European to have called the world's attention to the ruins of the temple of Angkor Vat one hundred years ago. Its monumental entrances and outer galleries are reached by causeways across a moat, 660 feet wide, that surrounds the entire rectangular enclosure. The waters of the moss-covered basin once formed a link in the intricate system of reservoirs and canals that brought life and fertility to the ancient Khmer capital.

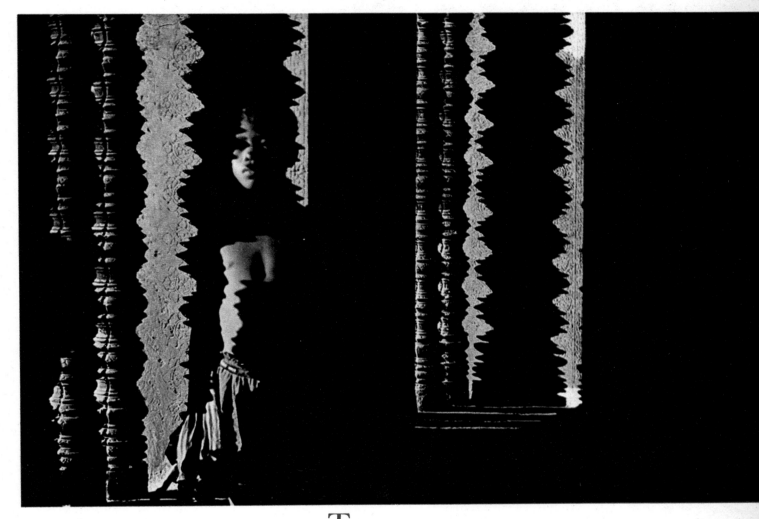

The voluted columns and balustrades above, reminiscent of natural growth, are characteristic of Angkor Vat. Once these galleries were peopled with robed priests and dignitaries. Now they are the refuge of bats that flit away at the approach of visitors such as this Cambodian boy.

At the midpoint of Angkor Vat's enclosure rises the temple's central mass (opposite), climbing tier by tier to a height of some two hundred feet. Towers surmount the galleries at all four corners, while at the center rises the tallest of them all—the sanctuary. Within its walls, sacred to the king and his priests, there was said to stand the statue of the god Vishnu, to whom the temple was dedicated. The shape of the towers derives from the lotus flower, symbol of the god who holds such a flower in each of his four hands.

Built later than the temple, the royal city of Angkor Thom shows a decadence of style; yet many consider its towers of Bayon the most powerful of the great Khmer monuments. On each of the four faces of these towers appears a head of the compassionate Buddha. From collar to crown, these massive images measure two yards. Below, a detail shows nature not only invading man's work but also complementing it. Lichens that overgrow the stone lend a patina to the sculptured Buddha, while the action of time adds strange effects in cleaving the unmortared blocks as new growth intrudes.

Overleaf:

The humanism introduced to Angkor by Buddhist feeling expresses itself in bas-reliefs that depict the people's daily life under Khmer civilization. The carvings shown, cut in sandstone in one of the interior galleries of Bayon, represent a procession of a Khmer king's army. A thirteenth-century Chinese envoy to Angkor, Chou Ta-Kwan, left a description that applies to portions of this relief: "When the king comes out, the troops are at the head of the procession. Their bodies and feet are bare. They hold a lance in their right hands and shields in the left. Then come the standards, the flags and the music. The king and the ministers are all mounted on elephants. In front of them many red parasols can be seen even from far off. Next come the wives and concubines of the king riding in palanquins, carts, or on horses and elephants. They carry more than one hundred parasols heavily decorated with gold. . . ."

Bayon bas-reliefs depict the Khmer as a warrior race. At the height of their twelfth-century power, they were invaded by their neighbors, the Chams of Annam. These figures are believed to be attacking Chams, wearing hats resembling inverted lotus.

In 1177, the Chams captured Angkor. To Chinese envoy Chou Ta-Kwan, the defeat of the Khmers came as no surprise since "there are neither bows nor arrows, bullets nor cannon balls, cuirasses nor helmets. . . . Generally these people know nothing of tactics or strategy."

The court of the Khmer king at Angkor was held twice daily, when the sovereign saw anyone who wanted an audience. Here a Bayon carving records a characteristic scene of courtiers and petitioners waiting upon the monarch.

Left and below: Details of royal processions at the height of Angkor's renown. The stiff formality of the court, and the elaborate trappings and ceremonials of such processions, moved visiting Chou Ta-Kwan to call the Khmers a nation of barbarians whose only knowledge was the worship of their king. Such carvings as these, however, with their elegance and sense of rhythm and form, belie the contemporary critic's disdain.

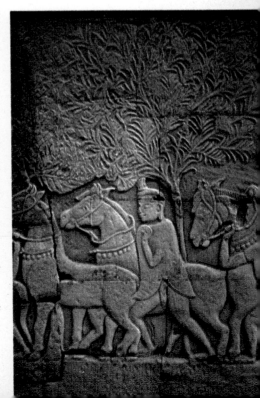

Above, a Buddhist priest of today in traditional robes visits the shrine of his ancestors.
Left, a figure of the celestial goddess, the Devata, gazes out over centuries from her niche.

In countless niches, amid tendrils of encroaching growth, appear carvings of graceful Devatas (left), with their spiral headdresses. At the time when these figures were being cut, cathedral-builders in Europe were decorating façades with comparable images. Above, a line of what are thought to be attendants of Buddha are seated in meditation.

Here, writes Osbert Sitwell, describing the interaction of man's work and nature at Angkor, "The stone itself acquires a kind of life from the struggle. . . . The interior has grown dark, starved and shrouded from this ceaseless combat, and under the force of it the numerous richly decorated reliefs have become endowed with a new if fortuitous power."

TEXT CONTINUED FROM PAGE 63

yards with the finicky exactitude of the detail and the decorations, that can embrace equally the self-contained perfection of an individual courtyard or building and still make it integral to the whole, that can grade the heights of the various structures from the low outer wall to the towering central shrine with a flawless sense of mounting grandeur to the most sacred temple, yet without ever slipping into the merely imposing or grandiose. It is a place and a moment to wonder at the overwhelming confidence and the assumption of expansive power that made those nameless architects of Angkor Vat plan a temple to occupy a site that is nearly a mile square in size.

One can try to imagine what Angkor Vat must have looked like when the Khmer priests and kings stared down from the pyramid upon the greatest temple in their kingdom nearly a thousand years ago. The courtyards must have been busy with people, with priests and worshipers, slaves and courtiers. Students and scholars must have been in and out of the libraries. From somewhere—one of the shrines—must have come the sound of religious chanting. Somewhere else a priest was surely leading a group of acolytes in a recitation of the scriptures. There was probably music summoning people to a service, or different music from a pavilion where the dancers were rehearsing. In one of the outer galleries there was probably a thriving little bazaar in progress because worshipers would certainly want flowers, fruit, and rice to place as offerings before the deities, and since, in Hinduism, a temple is a very intimate part of every side of a Hindu's life, there is nothing sacrilegious about buying and selling within the temple precincts. But in a second you contrast the picture in your mind with the dark gray stones below you where there is nothing, now, but death.

If Angkor Vat represents the height of the achievements of the Angkorean period, it is also a symbol of the finish of an empire. It seems incredible in retrospect that the building, carving, decorating, sculpturing of Angkor Vat was completed in about thirty years—one-third of the time that it took to construct one of the great Gothic cathedrals of Europe, which are mostly about a tenth the size. Yet in that fact itself is the most convincing clue to the destruction of Khmer rule and the disintegration of its power.

Jayavarman VII, the last of Cambodia's great "constructor kings," carried this passion for intensive building to the proportions of a mania. Hundreds of buildings were flung up with an almost frenzied speed to expand the royal capital. So far about six hundred have been discovered and at least partly restored, but scholars believe that there are still many more to be found—among them, colleges, libraries, palaces, monasteries, convents. There are long stone terraces, dominated by huge throne platforms, from which possibly Jayavarman VII reviewed his troops; there are elephant-mounting platforms, countless heroic and commemorative statues. And there are hospitals. Over each one are inscribed the words, "The ills of the people are the ills of their king. As the people suffer, so their king suffers . . ." From this and from other fragmentary evidence, the legend grew that Jayavarman VII was a leper and that the burst of building that he demanded from his people was intended to draw to him the compassion of the gods, a kind of bribe so that they would cure him.

It is after Jayavarman VII's reign that Angkor presents its greatest mystery. What became of the Khmers? They simply dropped out of history for no recorded reason. For many years it was assumed that some unknown wave of destruction had simply wiped the whole race out—plague, perhaps, or a change in the course of the rivers that forced a disorganized and deadly migration of the people. Actually, more recent researches provide a less dramatic but more reasonable explanation. The years of strain and pressure on the Khmers proved too much for the stamina of the people. Angkor slipped into a period of complacence, then of decline, and finally of decadence—an easy prey to its neighbor nations. The fourteenth century saw the start of a long series of attacks from Siam and from the coastal nations of Annam and Cochin China, and Cambodia was never again victorious against them. The gold and the treasures of Angkor were looted. Its royal dancers and musicians were taken captive and carried off to the court of Siam. Much of its sculpture, its images, its sacred deities were stolen. The provinces broke away, the empire dissolved. As the magnificence of Angkor disintegrated, the remaining people returned to the land to scratch a living however they could, leaving their great, lost capital to the encroaching jungle, allowing the slender trunks of the wild fig trees to break through the palaces, giving over their monuments to the corroding underbrush and their temples to the snakes and flights of bats.

Every now and again, as you travel in modern Cambodia, you will see on the face of a Cambodian villager a fleeting reminder of the idealized features of the Khmer sculptures. Quite often, in the countryside, as you watch a couple of men working a wooden water wheel, or a woman sifting rice, a boy with a bow and arrow, a young girl twisting flowers into her hair, you will find an echo of the Angkor bas-reliefs. Once, some years ago, Henri Marchal, one of the pioneer French archaeologists to explore and reconstruct Angkor, made this comment on the grand ideas of the old Khmers: "The people thought of their kings as gods and their gods as kings. And now—" he added sadly, "now our most eminent archaeologists cannot tell you whether these buildings are temples or tombs."

As the daughter of an Indian diplomat and as a novelist, Santha Rama Rau has traveled extensively exploring the cultural interactions of East and West. Her book, View to the Southeast, *published last year by Harper and Brothers, will be followed by* Russian Journey, *due for publication this spring.*

AN INTERVIEW BY GEORGE PLIMPTON

ERNEST HEMINGWAY

ON THE ART OF WRITING

This interview was conducted by George Plimpton, the leading spirit in the group of young Americans who founded *The Paris Review*. For their lively little magazine, which is published in France, Mr. Plimpton and his colleagues have interviewed a series of important literary figures; the results were published last spring in book form under the title *Writers at Work*, with an introduction by Malcolm Cowley. Hemingway, their biggest literary quarry, eluded them until after the collection was published. Mr. Plimpton then spent two weeks in Cuba, interviewing him at his home outside Havana.

HEMINGWAY: You go to the races?

INTERVIEWER: Yes, occasionally.

HEMINGWAY: Then you read the *Racing Form* . . . there you have the true Art of Fiction.

—*Conversation in a Madrid café, May, 1954*

Ernest Hemingway writes in the bedroom of his home in the Havana suburb of San Francisco de Paula. He has a special workroom prepared for him in a square tower at the southwest corner of the house, but prefers to work in his bedroom, climbing to the tower room only when "characters" drive him up there.

The bedroom is on the ground floor and connects with the main room of the house. The door between the two is kept ajar by a heavy volume listing and describing "The World's Aircraft Engines." The bedroom is large and sunny—the windows facing east and south letting in the day's light on white walls and yellow-tinged tile floor.

The room is divided into two alcoves by a pair of chest-high bookcases that stand out into the room at right angles from opposite walls. A large and low double bed dominates one section, oversized slippers and loafers neatly arranged at the foot, the two bedside tables at the head piled seven-high with books. In the other alcove stands a massive flat-top desk with two chairs at either side, its surface an ordered clutter of papers and mementos. Beyond it, at the far end of the room, is an armoire with a leopard skin draped across the top. The other walls are lined with white-painted bookcases from which books overflow to the floor and are piled on top among old newspapers, bullfight journals, and stacks of letters bound together by rubber bands.

It is on the top of one of these cluttered bookcases—the one against the wall by the east window and three feet or so from his bed—that Hemingway has his "work desk"—a square foot of cramped area hemmed in by books on one side and on the other by a newspaper-covered heap of papers, manuscripts, and pamphlets. There is just enough space left on top of the bookcase for a typewriter, surmounted by a wooden reading board, five or six pencils, and a chunk of copper ore to weight down papers when the wind blows in from the east window.

A working habit he has had from the beginning, Hemingway stands when he writes. He stands in a pair of his oversized loafers on the worn skin of a lesser kudu—the typewriter and the reading board chest-high opposite him.

When Hemingway starts on a project he always begins with a pencil, using the reading board to write on onion-skin typewriter paper. He keeps a sheaf of the blank paper on a clipboard to the left of the typewriter, extracting the paper a sheet at a time from under a metal clip that reads "These Must Be Paid." He places the paper slantwise on the reading board, leans against the board with his left arm, steadying the paper with his hand, and fills the paper with handwriting which through the years has become larger, more boyish, with a paucity of punctuation, very few capitals, and often the period marked with an "x." The page completed, he clips it face down on another clipboard which he places off to the right of the typewriter.

Hemingway shifts to the typewriter, lifting off the reading board, only when the writing is going fast and well, or when the writing is, for him at least, simple—dialogue, for instance.

He keeps track of his daily progress—"so as not to kid myself"—on a large chart made out of the side of a cardboard packing case and set up against the wall under the nose of a mounted gazelle head. The numbers on the chart showing the daily output of words vary from 450, 575, 462, 1250, to 512, the higher figures coming on days Hemingway puts in extra work so he won't feel guilty spending the following day fishing on the Gulf Stream.

A man of habit, Hemingway does not use the perfectly suitable desk in the other alcove. Though it allows more space for writing, it too has its miscellany: stacks of letters, a stuffed toy lion of the type sold in Broadway nighteries, a small burlap bag full of carnivore teeth, shotgun shells, a shoehorn, wood carvings of a lion, rhino, two zebras, and a wart hog—these last set in a neat row across the surface of the desk—and, of course, books. You remember books in the room, piled on the desk and bedside tables, jamming the shelves in indiscriminate order—novels, histories, collections of poetry, dramas, essays. A look at their titles shows their variety. On the shelf opposite Hemingway's knees as he stands up to his "work desk" are Virginia Woolf's *The Common Reader*, Ben Ames Williams' *House Divided*, *The Partisan Review*, Charles A. Beard's *The Republic*, Tarle's *Napoleon's Invasion of Russia*, *How Young You Look* by one Peggy Wood, Alden Brook's *Shakespeare and the Dyer's Hand*, Baldwin's *African Hunting and Adventure*, T. S. Eliot's *Collected Poems*, and two books on General Custer's fall at the Battle of the Little Big Horn.

The room, however, for all the disorder sensed at first sight, indicates on inspection an owner who is basically neat but cannot bear to throw anything away—especially if sentimental value is attached. One bookcase top has an odd assortment of mementos: a giraffe made of wooden beads; a little cast-iron turtle; tiny models of a locomotive, two jeeps, and a Venetian gondola; a toy bear with a key in its back; a monkey carrying a pair of cymbals; a miniature guitar; and a little tin model of a U.S. Navy biplane (one wheel missing) resting awry on a circular straw place mat. The quality of the collection is that of the odds and ends which turn up in a shoe box at the back of a small boy's closet. It is evident, though, that these tokens have their value, just as three buffalo horns Hemingway keeps in his bedroom have a value dependent not on size but on the fact that, during their acquisition, things went badly in the bush—which ultimately turned out well. "It cheers me up to look at them," Hemingway says.

Hemingway may admit superstitions of this sort, but he prefers not to talk about them, feeling that whatever value they may have can be talked away. He has much the same attitude about writing. Many times during the making of this interview he stressed that the craft of writing should not be tampered with by an excess of scrutiny—"that though there is one part of writing that is solid and you do it no harm by talking about it, the other is fragile, and if you talk about it, the structure cracks and you have nothing."

As a result, though a wonderful raconteur, a man of rich humor, and possessed of an amazing fund of knowledge on subjects that interest him, Hemingway finds it difficult to talk about writing—not because he has few ideas on the subject, but rather because he feels so strongly that such ideas should remain unexpressed, that to be asked questions on them "spooks" him (to use one of his favorite expressions) to the point where he is almost inarticulate. Many of the replies in this interview he preferred to work out on his reading board. The occasional waspish tone of the answers is also part of this strong feeling that writing is a private, lonely occupation with no need for witnesses until the final work is done.

This dedication to his art may suggest a personality at odds with the rambunctious, carefree Hemingway-at-play of popular conception. The point is, though, that Hemingway, while obviously enjoying life, brings an equivalent dedication to everything he does—an outlook that is essentially serious, with a horror of the inaccurate, the fraudulent, the deceptive, the half-baked.

Nowhere is the dedication he gives his art more evident than in the yellow-tiled bedroom, where early in the morning Hemingway gets up to stand in absolute concentration in front of his reading board, moving only to shift weight from one foot to another, perspiring heavily when the work is going well, excited as a boy, fretful, miserable when the artistic touch momentarily vanishes—slave of a self-imposed discipline that lasts until about noon, when he takes a knotted walking stick and leaves the house for the swimming pool where he takes his daily half-mile swim.

*   *   *

INTERVIEWER: Are these hours during the actual process of writing pleasurable?

HEMINGWAY: Very.

INTERVIEWER: Could you say something of this process? When do you work? Do you keep to a strict schedule?

HEMINGWAY: When I am working on a book or a story I write every morning as soon after first light as possible. There is no one to disturb you and it is cool or cold and you come to your work and warm as you write. You read what you have written and, as you always stop when you know what is going to happen next, you go on from there. You write until you come to a place where you still have your juice and know what will happen next and you stop and try to live through until the next day when you hit it again. You have started at six in the morning, say, and may go on until noon or be through before that. When you stop you are as empty, and at the same time never empty but filling, as when you have made love to someone you love. Nothing can hurt you, nothing can happen, nothing means anything until the next day when you do it again. It is the wait until the next day that is hard to get through.

INTERVIEWER: Can you dismiss from your mind whatever project you're on when you're away from the typewriter?

HEMINGWAY: Of course. But it takes discipline to do it and this discipline is acquired. It has to be.

INTERVIEWER: Do you do any rewriting as you read up to the place you left off the day before? Or does that come later, when the whole is finished?

HEMINGWAY: I always rewrite each day up to the point where I stopped. When it is all finished, naturally you go over it. You get another chance to correct and rewrite when someone else types it, and you see it clean in type. The last chance is in the proofs. You're grateful for these different chances.

INTERVIEWER: How much rewriting do you do?

HEMINGWAY: It depends. I rewrote the ending to *Farewell to Arms*, the last page of it, thirty-nine times before I was satisfied.

INTERVIEWER: Was there some technical problem there? What was it that had stumped you?

HEMINGWAY: Getting the words right.

INTERVIEWER: Is it the rereading that gets the "juice" up?

HEMINGWAY: Rereading places you at the point where it *has* to go on, knowing it is as good as you can get it up to there. There is always juice somewhere.

INTERVIEWER: But are there times when the inspiration isn't there at all?

HEMINGWAY: Naturally. But if you stopped when you knew what would happen next, you can go on. As long as you can start, you are all right. The juice will come.

INTERVIEWER: Thornton Wilder speaks of mnemonic devices that get the writer going on his day's work. He says you once told him you sharpened twenty pencils.

HEMINGWAY: I don't think I ever owned twenty pencils at one time. Wearing down seven No. 2 pencils is a good day's work.

INTERVIEWER: Where are some of the places you have found most advantageous to work? The Ambos Mundos Hotel must have been one, judging from the number of books you did there. Or do surroundings have little effect on the work?

HEMINGWAY: The Ambos Mundos in Havana was a very good place to work. This Finca is a splendid place, or was. But I have worked well everywhere. I mean I have been able to work as well as I can under varied circumstances. The telephone and visitors are the work destroyers.

INTERVIEWER: Is emotional stability necessary to write well? You told me once that you could only write well when you were in love. Could you expound on that a bit more?

HEMINGWAY: What a question. But full marks for trying. You can write any time people will leave you alone and not interrupt you. Or rather you can if you will be ruthless enough about it. But the best writing is certainly when you are in love. If it is all the same to you I would rather not expound on that.

INTERVIEWER: How about financial security? Can that be a detriment to good writing?

HEMINGWAY: If it came early enough and you loved life as much as you loved your work, it would take much character to resist the temptations. Once writing has become your major vice and greatest pleasure, only death can stop it. Financial security then is a great help as it keeps you from worrying. Worry destroys the ability to write. Ill-health is bad in the ratio that it produces worry which attacks your subconscious and destroys your reserves.

INTERVIEWER: Can you recall an exact moment when you decided to become a writer?

HEMINGWAY: No, I always wanted to be a writer.

INTERVIEWER: Philip Young in his

The master and the Cape buffalo: Hemingway in the workroom of his house in Havana where trophies, art works, and mountains of memorabilia surround him.

is to explore, but much of it and all that is irresponsible should not be written. Once written you have to stand by it. You may have said it to see whether you believed it or not. On the question you raised, the effects of wounds vary greatly. Simple wounds which do not break bone are of little account. They sometimes give confidence. Wounds which do extensive bone and nerve damage are not good for writers, nor anybody else.

INTERVIEWER: What would you consider the best intellectual training for the would-be writer?

HEMINGWAY: Let's say that he should go out and hang himself because he finds that writing well is impossibly difficult. Then he should be cut down without mercy and forced by his own self to write as well as he can for the rest of his life. At least he will have the story of the hanging to commence with.

INTERVIEWER: How about people who've gone into the academic career? Do you think the large numbers of writers who hold teaching positions have compromised their literary careers?

HEMINGWAY: It depends on what you call compromise. Is the usage that of a woman who has been compromised? Or is it the compromise of the statesman? Or the compromise made with your grocer or your tailor that you will pay a little more but will pay it later? A writer who can both write and teach should be able to do both. Many competent writers have proved it could be done. I could not do it, I know, and I admire those who have been able to. I would think, though, that the academic life could put a period to outside experience which might possibly limit growth of knowledge of the world. Knowledge, however, demands more responsibility of a writer and makes writing more difficult. Trying to write something of permanent value is a full-time job even though only a few hours a day are spent on the actual writing. A writer can be compared to a well. There are as many kinds of wells as there are writers. The important thing is to have good water in the well and it is better to take a regular amount out than to pump the well dry and wait for it to refill. I see I am getting away from the question, but the question was not very interesting.

CONTINUED ON PAGE 132

book on you suggests that the traumatic shock of your severe 1918 mortar wound had a great influence on you as a writer. I remember in Madrid you talked briefly about his thesis, finding little in it, and went on to say that you thought the artist's equipment was not an acquired characteristic, but inherited.

HEMINGWAY: Evidently in Madrid that year my mind could not be called very sound. The only thing to recommend it would be that I spoke only briefly about Mr. Young's book and his

trauma theory of literature. Perhaps the two concussions and the skull fracture of that year had made me irresponsible in my statements. I do remember telling you that I believed imagination could be the result of inherited racial experience. It sounds all right in good, jolly post-concussion talk, but I think that is more or less where it belongs. So until the next liberation trauma, let's leave it there. Do you agree? But thanks for leaving out the names of any relatives I might have implicated. The fun of talk

The legends that grew out of the Third Crusade never failed to recount the mutual respect that Richard and Saladin had for each other. This painting by the English artist Solomon Alexander Hart illustrates the scene described by Sir Walter Scott in The Talisman *of the purely imaginary visit paid by Saladin to the bedside of Richard during his prolonged illness. Disguised as an Arab physician, Saladin is about to give medication to the fever-ridden English monarch. The white-gowned Grand Master of the Templars and the stern crusader Sir Thomas of Gilsland, called De Vaux, fear to entrust their king's life to an infidel. Richard allays their suspicions as he grasps the physician's pulse: "His blood beats calm as an infant's, so throb not theirs who poison princes. De Vaux, whether we live or die, dismiss this Hakim with honor and safety. Commend us, friend, to the noble Saladin. Should I die, it is without doubt of his faith—should I live, it will be to thank him as a warrior would desire to be thanked." The two royal adversaries never actually met, but both prided themselves on their chivalrous code of warfare.*

Met in bloody war for the Holy Land, the champions of Christendom

and Islam gave the medieval world a lesson in the honor of kings

Richard and Saladin

By ALFRED DUGGAN

On June 8, 1191, King Richard Coeur de Lion joined the besiegers of Acre, who were themselves besieged by the great army of Saladin. He was thirty-three years old and already a veteran; since he was sixteen he had led armies. He was not only a brave knight but also a skilled commander, especially expert in siegecraft and in the dull business of looking after supplies. He was tall and fair and amazingly handsome; he was as well known for his poetry as for his courage, and he loved beauty in every form. He could inspire in his followers a lifelong devotion. But there were weaknesses in his character. His witty poet's tongue could say unforgivable things; in any company he must be first; he was stern, unyielding, truculent, and avaricious.

For two years he had been king of England, but his throne was not secure; John, his younger brother, would displace him if he could. Nonetheless, he and King Philip of France had sworn to reclaim the Holy Land together. After a winter spent in Sicily, and a detour by Richard to Cyprus (a conquest that later proved to be one of his shrewdest moves), they moved on separately to join the Third Crusade already in progress in Outremer on the Palestine coast.

On the European continent, France and England had been quarreling for a generation. Recently Richard had made matters worse by refusing to marry Philip's sister Alice, to whom he had been betrothed since childhood, giving as reason the rumors that she had been his father's mistress. To clinch the matter, Richard's mother brought Princess Berengaria of Navarre down to Sicily, and Richard married her on the island of Cyprus.

Relations between the two monarchs could scarcely have been worse. And although Richard had brought to Acre a finer body of troops and a larger sum of money than Philip, he could not command an army that contained the king of France because, as duke of Aquitaine, he had previously done homage to Philip. So Richard's intention was to clear up the mess in Outremer and get home as soon as possible, before trouble broke out in England.

However, the mess in Outremer presented many complications. Almost one hundred years earlier, in 1095, Pope Urban II had called upon Christian Europe to rescue the Holy Land from the infidels. In that First Crusade groups of Frankish and Norman knights had assembled large retinues, crossed Europe, fought their way through Asia Minor, and finally managed to wrest Jerusalem from its Egyptian rulers.

But these restless, ambitious adventurers had come to make their own fortunes as much as to restore the Holy Places. Each knight seized and secured what he could for himself, warring constantly with his Christian neighbors. Thus the Christian community was scarcely unified. It consisted principally of the kingdom of Jerusalem, which stretched from the Egyptian border to Beirut, and three associated states of Antioch, Tripoli, and Edessa, covering what is now Syria, Lebanon, and southeast Turkey. Edessa was retaken by the Moslems in 1144; its fall occasioned a second and wholly unsuccessful crusade.

Each of the remaining states was governed by hereditary descendants of the original knights, who carried on the feuds of their forebears. Toward the end of the twelfth century the king of Jerusalem, a leper, died childless, leaving two sisters whose marriages assumed supreme political importance. Sibylla, the elder sister, married Guy de Lusignan, a native of France, and they became king and queen of Jerusalem. Her teen-age half sister, Isabella, married Humphrey of Toron, the son of a native baron.

King Guy was heartily disliked by all of the local seigneurs because he was both ineffectual and a foreigner. The ensuing quarrels so weakened the Christian community that in 1187 Saladin, sultan of Egypt and Syria, marched upon the Christians at Hattin, captured King Guy, and destroyed most of the Christian forces. The Moslems then swept through Judaea, taking the Holy City and many castles of the hill country. When news of this disaster reached Europe, the Pope called for a third crusade.

By the end of the year, the Christians held only the seaport of Tyre, and that had been preserved by a strange stroke of luck. Its frightened defenders had already asked for terms when Conrad of Montferrat, arriving from Constantinople, rallied the city to hold out until reinforcements could save it. Conrad became thereby a local hero. Most of the lay barons through Outremer rallied to him, and it was suggested that he marry Princess Isabella, which would at least give him a rival claim to the throne of Guy and Sibylla.

Conrad was said to have left one wife in Italy and another in Constantinople; and Isabella's marriage to Humphrey of Toron was annulled rather against her will. She liked the gentle, charming young man who had been kind to her, and she did not at all fancy the rough old soldier. (Humphrey, who had homosexual leanings, had neglected to consum-

mate the marriage. Later he and Richard, who was rumored to be too fond of handsome young men, became close friends, which did not help matters.)

When King Philip of France reached Acre in April, 1191, six weeks before Richard, he encountered a strong movement to displace King Guy and make Conrad king of Jerusalem. The barons of the kingdom, sprung from French families, treated Philip as their natural lord; he in turn willingly supported their favorite, Conrad. Richard, upon arrival, backed Guy, partly because he refused to accept any of Philip's notions and partly because King Guy came from Richard's French domain of Poitou. Shortly thereafter a compromise was made whereby Guy would retain the crown during his lifetime (Sibylla had died without surviving issue), and Conrad would then assume the throne. This decision pleased no one and lasted only eight months.

Richard had other enemies. Because his sister Matilda was married to Henry the Lion, a hated foe of the Hohenstaufen emperors, the German Crusaders who preceded both the French and the English at Acre also distrusted him. Thus Richard went into battle with the French, most of the native barons, and the Germans all hostile to him for different reasons. His was not an enviable position.

But Saladin, encamped behind the besiegers of Acre, saw only that the Christian army had been reinforced by a mighty warrior. He made even greater efforts to relieve his blockaded city, for a great defeat might destroy his power. Saladin was a self-made sultan. He lacked the prestige of hereditary rule, and unless he led his men to victory and

A herald wearing the combined coat-of-arms of France and England welcomes two ladies to Sicily in 1190, where Richard and Philip spent the winter before journeying to the Holy Land. The women may be Richard's mother and his betrothed, Berengaria of Navarre.

The immediate cause of the Third Crusade was the fall of Jerusalem in 1187. Here Saladin, bedecked with crown and scepter, supervises the siege of the city walls. These illustrations from a French manuscript are based on the chronicles of the Christian crusader William of Tyre.

plunder they would desert him. His horsemen were Turks or Kurds (he was himself a Kurd); his foot, Sudanese; and his indispensable sappers and miners, Egyptian. All his soldiers hated the climate of the unhealthy coast, ravaged and stinking after four years of war. They would not stay unless they were paid punctually, and the money to pay them could come only from Egypt.

In 1191 Saladin was fifty-three and in poor health. But the Holy War was the great object of his life and, when his doctors warned him that a long stay in the hot plain would be fatal, he answered with a proverb: "Kill me and Malek, kill Malek with me." That had been spoken long ago by an Arab champion, struggling wounded on the ground with the leader of the enemy. Perhaps it had a more topical application, for in Arabic *el Malek* means "the King." Sixty years later, during the Crusade of St. Louis, Saracens would still say to a restive horse: "Do you think *el Malek* is after you?" They did not mean King Philip or King Guy; to Moslems *el Malek* could be no one but Richard, king of England.

Saladin had won his dominions in war, but he did not charge at the head of his troops. In battle his station was with the reserve; there is no record that he ever used his sword, save to kill unarmed prisoners after victory. Yet he was fearless, and if his army seemed to be beaten he would hold his ground to the last.

In every respect he was the pattern of a Moslem ruler. Though he never found time amid the cares of state to make the pilgrimage to Mecca, he said his prayers regularly and kept the Fast of Ramadan. He loved to listen to readings from the holy books, even while he rode down the front of a hostile army.

His almsgiving was so generous that when he died only one gold dinar remained in his treasury. To his subjects he was just, and even to Christians he kept his given word. His mercy was famous; but it was a Moslem mercy, not to be judged by Christian standards. When Jerusalem surrendered to him there were 60,000 Christian refugees in the town, and he set their ransom at the moderate figure of ten dinars a man. The money in the city treasury was reckoned toward this ransom, though Saladin might have claimed it as booty; to please his brother Saphadin, he freed a thousand captives and permitted the patriarch to beg off another seven hundred. Yet so many slaves remained that a pair of old shoes would buy a man.

While he lay before Acre, a Christian woman came from the crusaders' camp seeking audience with the sultan; she begged him to return her baby girl, stolen by Saracen soldiers. Saladin found the child, restored her to her mother, and returned both to the Christian camp—although he himself had organized this corps of Arab marauders.

As a young man he had served in the Egyptian civil wars alongside the army of Christian Jerusalem; it was said that he had been knighted by old Humphrey of Toron, grandfather of young Humphrey. He knew the type of behavior expected from Christian knights and, though he was not habitually chivalrous, he could answer chivalry in kind. When, in 1183, he suddenly attacked Kerak, that remote castle southeast of the Dead Sea was full of guests come to

Brutality was familiar to both Moslems and Christians during the fighting. Saladin's sense of honor did not prevent him from severing the head of Reynald of Châtillon with a stroke of his sword after that undisciplined lord had raided a rich Arab desert caravan.

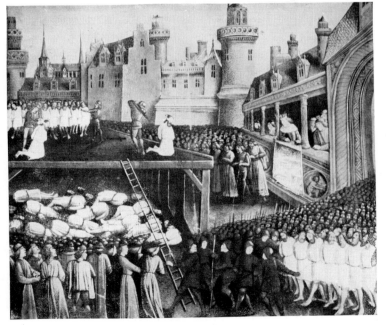

Such cruelty was outdone by Richard, who calmly watched the slaughter of 2,700 Moslem survivors in Acre after the city had been won by the Christians in the summer of 1191. The decapitated prisoners in their white robes are stacked beneath the wooden gallows.

89

the wedding of Humphrey of Toron and Princess Isabella. With cheerful defiance the chatelaine announced that since the great sultan had come to the wedding he must share in the feast; she sent out her servants with the best dishes and the best wine. In return Saladin gave orders that the tower which sheltered bride and bridegroom must not be bombarded.

We know nothing of Saladin's married life; but he had seventeen sons and at least one daughter, and took pains to bring them up properly. When the boys wished to join in a massacre of Christian prisoners he forbade it, explaining to his puzzled councilors that the children were too young to understand the true religion; if they were encouraged to kill helpless Christians, they might think it right to kill helpless Moslems.

When Richard reached the camp before Acre in June, 1191, the Moslem and Christian armies had been in close contact for three years, and truces were frequent, official or unofficial. It was natural that Richard, as soon as he arrived, should send envoys to Saladin; he was eager to meet the champion of Islam, who in a single battle had overthrown a kingdom. His first request was merely for an interview. Saladin answered that kings should not meet while they were at war, though if peace came he would be delighted to see him. Though Richard returned to this project more than once, the two leaders never met save on the battlefield, and never in single combat.

Richard was madly curious to learn more about his great antagonist. Again he sent his envoy, a Moroccan noble who had long been a captive in Christian hands (trustworthy interpreters were always hard to find). This time his mission was frivolous in the extreme. The envoy announced that Richard had some fine hawks that he would like to send as a present to Saladin; but the hawks were sick, and in the besieged camp of the besiegers of Acre they could not get the fresh food they needed. Would Saladin please send them some chickens?

Saladin willingly sent the poultry, though he said with a laugh that he knew Richard would eat them. He added a suggestion that any further envoys should be sent to Saphadin, his brother and the second lord in his dominions. Saladin may have been genuinely busy, or this may have been a barbed reminder that, while King Philip lay before Acre, Richard was only the second lord in the Christian army. Richard then asked if he might meet Saphadin. This request was granted, and a three-day truce was arranged to cover the interview. But Richard fell sick, like most other newcomers to the unhealthy coastal plain, and for the time being the project was abandoned.

Throughout July envoys passed to and fro. Richard sent the hawks and other Western curiosities; Saladin in return sent fruit and snow, precious luxuries in the blockaded camp. There was a sound political reason for these contacts.

The Moslem leaders in Acre were preparing to surrender, and Richard wished to make sure that Saladin knew it.

The surrender took place on July 12. King Philip promptly went home three weeks later to snatch at Richard's French holdings (and, some say, to intrigue with his brother John). In the tangled negotiations that followed, Richard spoke for the whole Christian army. The Moslems in Acre had offered to buy their lives by handing over three things which were not theirs to give: a large sum of money, the True Cross (captured at Hattin), and a hundred named Christian knights. Saladin eagerly collected the money; he was reluctant to hand over the True Cross, though he would probably have done so under pressure; but he failed to produce the named prisoners. On August 11 Richard's envoys refused to accept the money alone, though tempting sacks of gold were actually brought to their tent. On the twentieth, recognizing that the agreed ransom would never be handed over, Richard killed the Saracen soldiers in the surrendered garrison, along with their wives and children, to the number of 2,700, though a few wealthy emirs bought their lives by the offer of large individual ransoms. It is worth noting that, although modern historians reproach Richard, Saladin continued to negotiate and thought none the worse of him.

Having gained one impressive victory, Richard decided to march sixty miles south to Jaffa, which had fallen to the Moslems after Hattin. On September 5, during the march, Richard himself went out to Saphadin under a flag of truce. He offered to go home and leave the Moslems in peace— if Saladin would evacuate the whole kingdom of Jerusalem. He cannot have expected that his proposal would be accepted; but perhaps that was merely a convenient way of publishing his maximum demand on the eve of a great battle that he hoped would be decisive.

The Battle of Arsuf, on September 7, was indeed a Christian victory, although the Moslems were more frightened than hurt; the Turkish horse fled so fast that few were killed. But to Saladin it was a heavy blow. He ruled these men only because he led them to victory; if he made a habit of being beaten, as he had been beaten at Acre and Arsuf, they would find another sultan. Grimly he prepared to stand a siege in Jerusalem; for if he retired from that great conquest his army would desert him.

Richard delayed in Jaffa to secure a base of operations where he could receive supplies from his fleet. Also, he had been talking with the knights of his army, and it must suddenly have been brought home to him that he could not win the war. Every pilgrim was eager to assault the Holy City; but every pilgrim would go home as soon as he had prayed in the Holy Sepulchre. Jerusalem could not be held by the barons of the kingdom, split between Conrad and Guy, and their allies from Europe would not stay to help them. Richard, strong in the prestige of Arsuf, sat down to think out the best terms such prestige would bring him.

Wearing their crowns, King Philip II of France (left) and King Richard I of England
(right) set out from Vézélay on July 4, 1189, with their knights and infantry. This unity
of purpose temporarily halted the royal feuds that had kept France and England at war.

He chose a good envoy: Humphrey of Toron, the brave, epicene warrior whose grandfather had bestowed on the youthful Saladin the girdle of knighthood. Humphrey spoke Arabic well and needed no interpreter; Saphadin knew and liked him, and Saphadin was nearby at Lydda.

To Saphadin, Humphrey propounded a reasonable compromise. Let Saladin retire from Jerusalem and the western half of the kingdom, as far as the line of the Jordan; and the True Cross, of no value to Saladin, should be returned. Saladin also had been thinking things over. The coastal plain was deadly, not only to himself but to his army; he began to see that he would never conquer the Christian ports. In his answer to Richard, Saladin said that he would never yield Jerusalem. (Perhaps he managed to convey that he dared not, lest such a retreat should cost him his throne.) Though one day he might return the True Cross, the great

prize must be dearly bought. Yet he still wished for peace. Could Richard make another offer?

Richard answered with a plan for the neutralization of the Holy Places, a plan quite unmedieval in its practical forethought. But since this was still the twelfth century, the foundation of the scheme was a royal marriage. Richard had with him in Jaffa his sister Joan, the widowed queen of Sicily. He offered to make over to her his conquests in Outremer, the strip of land he had conquered between Tyre and Ascalon. Let Saladin give his brother the whole of Palestine; then Joan should marry Saphadin. The plan was worked out in elaborate detail. The royal pair would reign in Jerusalem, which would be open to pilgrims of every faith; in each town there would be separate Moslem and Christian quarters; all prisoners held by either side should be freed without ransom; the Templars and Hospital-

CONTINUED ON PAGE 130

91

The Future of Machine Civilization

As the earth's easily available resources are used up, our industrial order is nearing a point of no return. Barring disaster, it can prosper on little more than sea water and granite. But if it should be destroyed in a world cataclysm, it might never rise again

By HARRISON BROWN

Civilized man is coming to the point at which, for his own survival, he will be dependent upon the smooth functioning of his machines. Up to now in human history, this has not been true. Machines have been simply labor-saving devices, rather pleasant luxuries, which enabled us to substitute the energy of coal for the beast of burden or for human muscle. But the role of machines in civilization is undergoing a transformation and we shall, in the not too distant future, become their slaves. We must continue feeding them; we must keep them operating; we must build new ones at an accelerating pace. If for any reason they were collectively to fail us, the kind of civilization we know would come to an end and many of us would perish.

Prophets of the future often assume that, even in the event of such a catastrophe, a new industrial civilization would some day rise from the ruins. But this is probably a false comfort. The fact is that we are rapidly approaching a point where such a process of reconstruction would be difficult—if not impossible.

The reason, though seldom given much consideration in discussions of man's future on this planet, is really quite simple. Our present machine civilization was built by mak-

ing use of the mineral resources easily available on or near the earth's surface. Within a period of time that is very short compared with the total span of human history, supplies of fossil fuels will almost certainly be exhausted. This loss will make man completely dependent upon water power, atomic energy, and solar energy (including that made available by burning vegetation) for driving his machines. There are no fundamental physical laws that prevent such a transition, and it is quite possible that society will be able to make the change smoothly. But it is a transition that will happen only once during the lifetime of the human species.

Once we have crossed the fateful divide, our technology will permit us to continue for as long as industrial civilization keeps functioning. But if for any reason disaster strikes and the industrial network is destroyed, easily available mineral resources—the building blocks of the Industrial Revolution—will not be there for man to use. Without them it seems doubtful that we shall ever again be able to lift ourselves above the agrarian level of existence. Thus man may well be approaching, in terms of industrial civilization, a "point of no return."

Machine civilization as we know it is a manifestation of a

NICHOLAS N. SOLOVIOFF

new stage of evolution of living matter on earth. Since the dawn of life, the earth has been the abode of innumerable complex interlocking networks of living things, each of which was molded by the combination of the environment and the biological innovations which had appeared up to that time.

Man is the most recent successful arrival on the evolutionary scene. With the help of his machines, he has achieved an unprecedented degree of dominance in the biological environment. But, like the amphibians and the reptiles before him, his continued prosperity is not assured by nature.

Man emerged into the world a million or so years ago and for a large part of that time he lived much like the other animals about him. But this new creature possessed a power that was unique on the world scene—the power of conceptual thought. This capability released him from the bondage of being primarily dependent upon instinct. He could benefit from the accumulated knowledge of his ancestors. He could transmit his own store of knowledge in detail to his offspring.

With the help of this power, man spread to all the parts of the earth where he could eke out an existence. Eventually about ten million human beings inhabited the earth, obtaining their sustenance by hunting and fishing and by gathering varieties of edible plants. That was as far as man could go in terms of numbers until his accumulated knowledge permitted him to obtain more food than was provided by the earth in its natural state. The undeveloped land was then saturated with humanity.

About seven thousand years ago, a dramatic invention appeared that was destined greatly to enhance man's dominance. Man learned that he could cultivate edible plants, and this made it possible for hundreds of men to live on land that previously supported only one or two. It became possible for an individual to produce more food than he needed for himself and his family, and thus the way was paved for the emergence of towns and civilizations. Human

populations increased rapidly. By A.D. 1650 there were perhaps fifty times as many human beings as had existed in preagricultural days—about 500 million in all.

Throughout the greater part of the agricultural revolution, work was done almost entirely by domesticated animals and by human beings. However, large quantities of wood were consumed for cooking, house-heating, brick-making, and metallurgical purposes. Indeed, the second dramatic "breakthrough" in mankind's history was brought about directly by the fact that the forests in many parts of the world had been cut down.

In England, coal came into widespread use as a substitute for wood. But there was one important process in which wood could not be replaced. Iron manufacture depended upon charcoal, which was made from wood, and repeated attempts to produce an equivalent of charcoal from coal met with failure. Eventually, however, processes were discovered for converting coal into coke, which was a satisfactory charcoal substitute, and the iron industry was liberated from its dependence upon woodlands.

The linking of coal to iron was one of the most fateful achievements in mankind's history. It precipitated a series of rapid developments in the course of which a principle that we now call "feedback" exerted profound effect.

As iron became more readily available it came to be more widely used. The demand for coal increased rapidly, with the result that the miners had to dig ever deeper underground. Ground water became a major problem in mining, and efforts to cope with it led to the development of a crude steam engine that could drive a water pump and that operated on coal. Further development of this early engine led to its being used for other purposes. It was soon applied in the textile industry, then for transportation. These developments in turn led to increased demands for both iron and coal. The demand for machines grew, as did the demand for machines for making machines.

From those early beginnings, industrial civilization

93

emerged in Western Europe. Soon it spread to North America. Later it spread eastward to Russia and westward to Japan. Today we see it spreading to China and India. Barring an intervening catastrophe, it seems inevitable that machine culture, like agriculture, is destined one day to become world-wide.

In the Western world, once machine culture became deeply rooted, developments followed each other with incredible rapidity. The combination of adequate nourishment and the rapid expansion of medical research and public-health techniques raised average life expectancy at birth from fifty years in 1900 to nearly seventy years in 1950. Scientists, inventors, and engineers designed an accelerated flow of new products, devised new production techniques, and greatly increased output per man-hour. Working hours were reduced, and the flow of goods per capita continued to increase rapidly. It began to appear that the combination of science, engineering, and industry might eventually transform the world into a paradise where everyone would have enough to eat, where individuals might own practically all of the material goods they might possibly desire.

However, just as the human body cannot survive on air alone, an industrial machine must be provided with energy and with raw materials if it is to survive. Our industrial civilization feeds on huge quantities of raw materials such as phosphate rock, sulfur, water, and ores of iron, copper, and aluminum. And just as the human body requires energy in the form of food, so our industrial network requires energy in the form of fuels such as coal, natural gas, and petroleum.

As per capita demand for goods continues to grow, as population increases, and as industrialization spreads to other regions of the world, the demand for raw materials will surge upward. Each decade we must produce more materials than were produced the decade before; we must produce more fertilizers, insecticides, machines, and medicines. Correspondingly, we must consume more ores, more coal, more petroleum.

But the ores that feed our machines are not renewable. They were deposited by nature over periods of millions of years and are not being replaced at any appreciable rate today. This means that as time goes by, we will be forced to process ores of steadily lowering grade, and we will be forced to dig ever deeper into the earth. This process of depletion will continue until ores as such no longer exist.

When civilization reaches the point when there are no longer any ores, can it continue to function? We now know that it can, for if necessary our machines could feed successfully on the leanest of earth substances—ordinary rock, sea water, air, sedimentary deposits of limestone and phosphate rock, and sunlight.

We can expect that the industries of the world as a whole will pass through several stages, at the end of which time mineral resources will cease to be important factors in world economy. As high-grade ores diminish in abundance, we will consume our energy resources more rapidly. As coal dwindles and becomes more expensive, its use will be reserved for premium functions such as reducing iron ore and producing organic chemicals. Eventually iron will be produced entirely without coal, by reduction with hydrogen in electric furnaces, and coal will be reserved entirely for the production of chemicals. At some time in the future, aluminum will be produced in the main from anorthosites and clays. Consumption of magnesium will increase, partly as the result of its ready availability in sea water. Sulfuric acid will be produced entirely from calcium sulfate. Increasing emphasis will be placed on the utilization of nitric and hydrochloric acid, largely as the result of the ready availability of raw materials for both. Minor elements such as copper, tin, lead, nickel, and germanium will be extracted from ores containing lower and lower concentrations of the elements, and increasing emphasis will be placed on the extraction of co-products, among which costs can be divided, and on the utilization of substitutes. The mining industries as we know them today will be transformed into enormous chemical industries.

Eventually the time will come when ordinary rocks such as granite will be looked upon as ores. One hundred tons of average igneous rock contain, in addition to other useful elements, 8 tons of aluminum, 5 tons of iron, 1,200 pounds of titanium, 180 pounds of manganese, 70 pounds of chromium, 40 pounds of nickel, 30 pounds of vanadium, 20 pounds of copper, 10 pounds of tungsten, and 4 pounds of lead. Given adequate supplies of energy, these elements could be extracted from the rock, and we now know that the rock itself contains the requisite amount of energy in the form of uranium and thorium.

One ton of average granite contains about four grams of uranium and about twelve grams of thorium. These are admittedly tiny amounts, but the energy content of this amount of uranium and thorium is equivalent to the energy released by burning approximately fifty tons of coal. The actual processing of the rock can be accomplished at an energy expenditure considerably smaller than fifty tons of coal, with the result that it is possible to obtain a net energy profit from average rock and at the same time obtain a variety of metals that are essential to the operation of an industrial society.

The basic raw materials for the industries of the future thus will be sea water, air, ordinary rock, sedimentary deposits of limestone and phosphate rock, and sunlight. All the ingredients essential to a highly industrialized society are present in the combination of those substances.

A great deal of water will be distilled from the sea for agricultural and industrial purposes, and most food will be grown using artificial fertilizers. Metals such as iron, aluminum, titanium, manganese, copper, tungsten, and lead will be obtained from rock, which raw material will also

CONTINUED ON PAGE 128

94

By ELEANOR C. MUNRO

MONSIEUR BERTIN *by J. A. D. Ingres*

PORTRAITS IN OUR TIME

The age-old contest between artist and sitter enlivens a new boom

Jean Auguste Dominique Ingres was the most brilliant portrait painter of his day. Napoleon sat for him; so did the Duke of Orléans and the intellectual elite of Italy and France. But his agony over these commissions was famous. An apocryphal story is told about a distinguished editor, Monsieur Bertin, whose sessions before the master had dragged on for months. Finally Ingres slammed down his crayon, announcing that he washed his hands of the whole business. "*Quoi!*" croaked Bertin, clapping his hammy hands to his knees in exasperation. "*Tiens!*" cried the artist, "The pose at last!" And thereupon he finished the picture, one of his greatest, in no time at all.

The question that beset Ingres is at the very heart of modern portraiture. What is likeness, he asks, and how can it be found? If it is only the face, then any educated painter can set it down. Ingres threw away hundreds of respectable sketches en route to the last. Upon technical know-how, pure and simple, a quite lucrative modern portrait industry is built.

But if likeness includes the breath of life, and all the vaporous ghosts which modern psychology has flushed out— if it includes even the face of a nation and an epoch—then something more than technique is called for. There are a few serious painters today who include portraiture among their other experiments. But these artists share very little with the commercial portraitists: neither goals nor, unfortunately, financial security.

Classical portraiture depended on an amiable kind of truce between the artist and his sitter. The subject refrained from making finicky demands, and the painter agreed that his first job was to present the facts. He squinted along his brush to size up the body, mixed and remixed colors to match the precise hue of the eyes. Then, once he had set down a skeleton of reality, he was more or less free to make his own comments, as Goya did in his devastating Spanish portraits.

But when classical principles break down, the confusion about likeness can erupt. Michelangelo, as the Renaissance world was crumbling, scornfully turned his back on portraiture. Reproached for not making his Medici tomb figures into correct likenesses, he scoffed that in a century no one would know the difference. Three hundred years later, Ingres trumpeted a new era of revolution. All his brilliant classical draftsmanship only helped him along the way. The *moment juste* had to be pounced upon, like an enemy agent.

The French Revolution had sapped classical portraiture of its lifeblood of rich, rather narcissistic noblemen with time on their hands. Another blow to the art was given, only five

95

years after Ingres painted Bertin, by the invention of the daguerreotype process. The camera became the rage of the nineteenth century. It was ingratiatingly cheap and quick, and its tricky kind of truth was a revelation. Delacroix, a bitter enemy of Ingres' classicism, said that beside a photograph of the naked human body even a Raphael looked out of kilter.

Suddenly, artists realized that no brush could copy a true likeness. The very eye of a painter lied to him; his heart swerved his brush. This shocking insight was like a reef on which the art of portraiture broke into pieces.

At first, even the conventional portrait industry foundered. In the New World, country limners and "fancy painters" lost their trade to the photographers. In Europe, there were soon no more customers for those fastidious miniatures on ivory or wood that had been family heirlooms since the time of Elizabeth I. But, like many other services, commercial portraiture revived on the wave of prosperity in our time. Today it commands high fees and an impressive roster of artists, though it still cannot compete with the most famous portrait boom in history, that in seventeenth-century Holland. Then so many painters sweated to supply the newly rich burghers in their spanking mansions that surplus production had to be auctioned off, given away in lotteries, and sold at market like tulip bulbs.

Commercial portraits today are channeled through grave establishments like Portraits, Incorporated, in New York and other galleries from coast to coast and in Europe. Through these, a prospective sitter can be matched to an artist whose manner and mood complement his own. Many artists are specialists, either in children or retiring chairmen of company boards. These are the two favorite categories. Beautiful women clamored loudest for portraits for five hundred years; now grandmothers and committees assigned by boards of trustees do most of the shopping. As one might expect, neither of these groups is particularly adventurous in its taste. The kind of portraits they choose tend on the one hand to a kind of breathless sweetness, and on the other, to a look of well-adjusted complacency.

Lately, a few families have begun to order "conversation pieces." Simon Elwes' luncheon scene (page 105) and Franklin Watkins' impression of the De Schauensee children (page 100) show how successful this genre can be. Decorous and gentle, it can suggest a kind of warm domesticity that a camera, with its hard eye for fact, could hardly achieve without fancy lighting effects. This is a vein in which a few original and gifted artists work. In return, they demand a certain *laissez faire* from the sitters.

The majority of the painters exploit hesitant little currents of style as they filter down from the radical inventions

This portrait of Jane, Lady Dalkeith, so delighted the Selection Committee of the British Royal Academy in 1958 that all fourteen members joined in giving it an "A" rating—an honor, according to one academician, not awarded since "before our time."

John R. Merton, the artist, was commissioned by Lord Dalkeith to paint his beautiful bride for the drawing room of Eildon, the family's seat in Melrose, Scotland. Merton's method of work is novel. Placing his subject in a stationary chair, he seats himself in

a dental operating chair on wheels. "In this way," he says, "I can work very close for painting in great detail and push myself back, without getting up, to obtain the general effect." Lady Dalkeith sat for fifty hours. "She has an enchanting smile," says Merton, "and since I did not feel I could paint the main portrait smiling I thought of the statuettes as a device for introducing other aspects of her. The book she holds bears the coat of arms of the Scott family, the motto Amo, the date, and her name. The heraldic device over her head represents the heart of King Bruce being carried on wings. The heart was in fact brought back from the Holy Land by a Douglas ancestor of Lord Dalkeith's. In the background are the Eildon hills and a bend in the river Tweed, a favorite view of Sir Walter Scott's."

To critics who dismiss his work as "candy-box painting," Merton replies that he paints subjects of his own choice, and his own choice is usually a beautiful woman.

of avant-garde painting. William Draper's manner is brushy and loose; he strokes his paint directly onto the primed canvas, sketching out the big shadows and high lights of a face as though he were painting a sunshiny landscape. Other artists use a tight, perfectionist hand, shaping hard, clear outlines, ivory-smooth skin which shines sleekly, and impeccable details picked out across the costume. Lately, the splashy, casual, but immensely elegant style of John Singer Sargent has begun to appeal: Aaron Shikler is a young Sargentesque portraitist. His light-streaked subject shown on page 101 gleams with melancholy drama against its warm backdrop.

Prices vary. For $150, many artists will deliver a simple drawing or pastel study of a head; $10,000 will buy a full-length, immaculately finished masterwork by the Anglo-American society painter Gerald Brockhurst, whose sitters have included Astors, Mellons, and Marlene Dietrich.

All kinds of tricks and ruses have been devised by portrait artists to extract that subtle emanation of personality which it took Ingres months to evoke. The Englishman John Merton, for instance, takes photographs of his sitter, then shuffles through them, picking out the best for use as aids. In America, Brockhurst offers music on a record player to help his sitter relax, though he says that at home in England a whisky produced the same effect. When commissioned to paint Dr. C. W. Mayo, William Draper even went so far as to put on a mask and follow his subject to the operating table. He was so struck by the surgeon's performance there that he painted him where he stood, by a wash-up sink, in rubber gloves and sterile gown (page 104).

Sometimes the artist himself is called on to perform operations—the equivalent of what plastic surgeons call "cosmetic procedure"—and to remove scars and moles, raise ears, or shave down a nose.

America's portrait fashion at the moment calls for a very informal kind of costume. Some families even pose in jodhpurs or shorts. The rare middle-aged woman sitting for a portrait often wants to be painted in street dress. This seems a pity. Gloves and feathers, jewels and great shawls helped many painters in the past to make brilliant compositions out of what might have been commonplace ones. Is this reticence due to the fact that "dressing up" has come to be synonymous with pretension? Even in sixteenth-century England, when manners were still relatively primitive, it delighted the Tudor nobles to dress up in starched and

Salvador Dali painted this remarkable likeness of his friend and patron, Chester Dale, one of America's foremost art collectors. The portrait was begun two years ago when Mr. and Mrs. Dale, with their poodle, visited Dali at his home at Port Lligat, Spain; it was finished in New York. The cliff and the stone tower belong to the Costa Brava, but nothing in the landscape recalls the earlier Dali world of limp watches and stomach clocks. The portrait demonstrates that even today a speaking likeness can be a work of art.

embroidered robes for their portraits. And those same Dutch burghers whose taste in interior décor ran to whitewash and blue delft, put on stiff ruffs and whalebones, buckled shoes and lace cuffs when they posed for their once-in-a-lifetime portrait. It is not only to our modern eyes that these costumes have a decorative charm, for the effect was quite conscious.

Nor do men and women today want to seem awe-inspiring. They would rather look good-natured than serious, friendly than sharp-witted. The artist is driven into a corner: Brockhurst says he has learned what a client means when he asks casually, "Don't I look rather intense here?"

There remains one way today of conveying great splendor palatably, and that is in a historical mold. Pietro Annigoni and John Merton are masters of this device, which appeals especially to British and Italian café society and aristocracy. Both painters use Florentine Renaissance brushwork and slick paint surface. In their paintings, it is the style that impresses, not the qualities of the sitters, who may be quite as undemonstrative as the average client in this country.

Whatever manner it chooses to assume as fashions shift, documentary portraiture of the commercial kind depends on technical tour de force. It represents the world as the world likes to see itself. It has rather little to do with that art of portraiture that has rendered not only the face and costume but the very heart of individual men and women and, indirectly, of their worlds.

That kind of probing, questioning art began some 3,000 years before Christ among the stonecarvers of Egypt. In those days portraits were intended to be reflections of the soul of a man. After his death, the tall, staring spirit-statue of him was walled into his tomb along with the painted mummy case. There the granite image stood, awaiting a day when the bodyless spirit in heaven might feel homesick for the fragrance of flowers and smoking beef-sides and slip down like a fiddler crab into its stony shell. And these were astonishingly accurate portraits too. Some years ago, as one of them was being taken from its tomb, the native diggers suddenly fell on their faces crying, "The mayor! The mayor of our village!" There, overleaping the ages, stood the image of the local mayor; and it is labeled by his name in the Cairo Museum today.

Not every great age produced portraits: the Greeks made almost none, except on their coins, until the time of Alexander the Great, whose legions ranged over the world from India to Egypt. Alexander had his own private portrait artist, the sculptor Lysippus. That master unconsciously paralleled Alexander's amazing conquest of space: he changed the rules of proportion that classical Greece had set down, stretching up his figures to seven instead of six heads high. His portraits of the Emperor show wide-open eyes, hair streaming like feathers, and a bone structure that became the ideal of beauty for the Hellenistic world. It was even taken over for the first groping images of Christ.

TEXT CONTINUED ON PAGE 102

THE MISSES DE SCHAUENSEE AND MUFFIN *by Franklin C. Watkins*

DANNY FILLIN *by Alexander Brook*

The charming evocation of childhood at left and the young boy above were both painted by well-established American painters. Restless children can be a problem, but Franklin Watkins finds "they throw off a meaning and a character as they flit by which is indispensable." Alexander Brook declares they are his most inspiring subjects because they force quick observation.

Experimentalists of the younger generation, like Larry Rivers, also do portraits when they are commissioned by adventurous patrons. In this case, the subject decided against having the image that resulted (below) gazing at her from her wall, and bought another Rivers painting instead.

Aaron Shikler is a realist who paints landscapes, still lifes, and figures as well as portraits. His elegant canvas of Mrs. Morrow, a fashion model and wife of the band leader Buddy Morrow, is reminiscent of John Singer Sargent.

MRS. HENRY FEDER *by Larry Rivers*

MRS. MUNI MORROW *by Aaron Shikler*

One of the bravest sitters a painter ever had is surely Mrs. Leigh Block. An attractive woman, as the photograph above indicates, Mrs. Block is the wife of a Chicago steel executive and a knowing patron and collector of art. It was, therefore, with eyes wide open that she commissioned Ivan Le Lorraine Albright to paint her portrait. Albright, who is famed for painting human flesh that looks as if it had been six weeks in the grave, required Mrs. Block to sit for him two to five times a week for two years. The result is shown at left. Mrs. Block says she is pleased with it.

TEXT CONTINUED FROM PAGE 99

But it is in the faces of republican Rome that we first recognize our ancestors. These iron-willed, impassive men are the founding fathers of the Western world. Every line and wrinkle is drawn upon these marble busts, even the pouchy eye and the puritanical squint. In our own Republic's early wilderness, among the hills of Connecticut and Pennsylvania, journeymen artists with their paintpots and pattern books saw and set down the same expressions.

There followed centuries when the individual was swallowed up by whirlpools of barbarian invasions. It was not until the medieval world was crumbling that portraits were made again. Then the art flourished first in the damp and busy Netherlands. There hundreds of painters bent over their small wooden panels, painting in an intriguing new material—oil—the burghers of rich wool centers like Bruges and Antwerp.

But in a much humbler material was painted one of the first faltering portraits which tried to express a man's spirit. It was painted not even from life, but as police artists do today—from eyewitness reports. The figure, sad-eyed and mouse-faced, drawn in grayish fresco on the walls of the lower church of Assisi, is Saint Francis, whose gentle preachings foreshadowed the Renaissance. He was drawn there probably by a Florentine artist named Cimabue, whose greater claim on history is as the teacher of Giotto. And between Giotto and Ingres, almost every Western artist painted portraits.

One of the first who set out to "flatter" a client was Piero della Francesca. A nuptial portrait was wanted for the swashbuckling *condottiere*, Federigo da Montefeltro. Unfortunately, he had been disfigured in battle. A lance had struck him across the face, destroying one eye and making a notch in the bridge of his nose. So Piero turned the bridegroom to his good side and painted a humped and beaked nose that is almost an emblem of Renaissance heroism.

Portraiture became a kind of romantic metaphor expressing a painter's own vision: Leonardo's smiles, with their labyrinths of meaning; Titian's tranquil, sumptuous princes; the tragical dwarfs of Velazquez; the eroded faces Rembrandt mined from the Amsterdam ghetto, along with the images of himself. At last, in the late eighteenth century, style called up a procession of rococo courtesans, dressed in the latest fashion as Roman vestal virgins and Dianas of the hunt. It was that same rococo that drained the treasuries of the three Louises, bringing about revolutions and the modern world.

Henceforth, the taste-makers would be geniuses of mechanics and industry, including Daguerre. There were, of course, a few pioneers who used Daguerre's invention in daring new ways. Mathew B. Brady recorded the grizzled faces of Civil War soldiers and their wan, pinch-waisted girls; David Octavius Hill, his hard-bitten Scottish countrymen. The Parisian Nadar took his camera up in a balloon and down into a coal mine. In between, he settled in his studio making portrait photos of Delacroix, Balzac, and other vanguard fighters for the new styles of Romanticism and Realism.

For their part, many serious painters after Delacroix gave up all hope of painting the kind of portrait likenesses they now critically labeled "photographic." These artists tore their subjects apart and then reassembled the features. They speckled points of pure color over a field of flesh; they dragged their brushes through great clots of paint, then drew faces wobbly with terror or ecstasy, like faces in a dream. The most fascinating modern portraits are this kind of private, groping study: Manet's model, her face blasted by sunlight; Cézanne's wife; Van Gogh's own wretched visage, a bandage over the mutilated ear. Picasso and Matisse tortured the likeness even further, into splinters of brown pigment or flat splotches of crimson and green.

"Even such things as the note of a person's voice, I have found immensely haunting in re-enacting his personality on canvas," says Graham Sutherland, the English semi-abstract painter of thorn bushes and Crucifixions. Also as battlegrounds for his own operations, he has used two of the most formidable faces of our time: Churchill's and Maugham's. "I think the portrait the most difficult genre in all art," Sutherland says, for "the painter is trying to extract the real personality of the sitter, and the sitter, nine times out of ten, is trying to withhold what he thinks one will get."

When Sir Winston Churchill received this painting as a gift on his eightieth birthday, he eyed it coldly and allowed that "it certainly combines force and candor." Some of his admirers were less restrained: "It makes him look like an evil, bilious toad," said one. The portrait had been painted on commission from the British Parliament by Graham Sutherland, whose fine portrait of Somerset Maugham appears on page 107. Somewhat taken aback by the critical reception given to his Churchill by the public, Sutherland commented ruefully: "People have their own conception of what a national hero should look like." Certainly the Sutherland portrait seems unlikely to replace the famous "bulldog" photograph by Karsh (right) as a public image of hero Churchill.

103

COUNTESS PAOLA VENEROSI-PESCIOLINI *by Pietro Annigoni*

SUNDAY LUNCH AT PEACOCK POINT *by Simon Elwes*

DR. C. W. MAYO *by William F. Draper*

Important people of wealth and fame comprise a staple of the international portrait market. The Florentine painter Annigoni, who painted the Italian beauty above, is one of the most expensive portraitists today. Clients admire his impeccable Renaissance technique. William F. Draper, who painted Dr. Mayo of the Mayo Clinic, is one of the busiest of the painters who work through Portraits, Inc., the New York clearing house for artists and clients.

Above right, the "conversation piece" by the British painter Simon Elwes represents a type of group portrait that was popular in eighteenth-century England, and that is now having a revival. The painting shows the traditional family Sunday lunch at the Locust Valley, Long Island, home of Mrs. Henry P. Davison, widow of a former president of J. P. Morgan & Company, who is at the far end of the table. Mr. Elwes, who paints single portraits as well as groups, gave this painting to the Davisons in gratitude for their having provided a home in America for his children during the war. To carry out the complicated composition, Elwes spent many hours in this pleasant dining room, painting all sixteen members of the family.

When the sitter wins, the portrait, in Sutherland's own words, can be "masklike: Churchill had very definite feelings as to how he should look as a man of destiny." On the other hand, when the painter wins, the result can be as disquieting as Ivan Albright's Mrs. Block (see page 102).

And yet, now as always, there is the possibility of arranging that classical truce between a courageous patron and a painter under which the art of portraiture once flourished. There are young realist painters of Aaron Shikler's circle; abstract expressionists around Larry Rivers; magic realists like Andrew Wyeth; and sensitive personalities like Milton Avery, Fairfield Porter, and others. All these artists—and others whose names can be had from museums and local galleries—from time to time accept portrait commissions. Their portraits are not always guaranteed to please, like those of their more practiced commercial colleagues. But from the encounter some greater surprise may emerge.

In the National Gallery in Washington, D.C., hang portraits of all those millionaires who wagered for immortality by buying up treasures around the world and establishing this great museum. Andrew Mellon is there, and Samuel H. Kress, and Chester Dale, in another painting than the one by Dali which is reproduced here. But many visitors pass these by to stare at the strange, attenuated, El Greco-like visage of Philadelphia's Joseph E. Widener. For, instead of the fashionable portraitists whom some of his fellow-donors hired, Widener had the courage to sit for an unconventional English romanticist, Augustus John.

Goethe said that one is never satisfied by the portrait of a person one knows. So much more of the artist himself than of the sitter lies in a portrait, in every exaggerated feature, every over-stressed shade. And yet one soon forgets to be dissatisfied with a great portrait. Before long, it becomes history; and then the sitter's ghost may be flattered by a quite different kind of immortality than even he had sought.

Eleanor C. Munro, art historian and critic, is on the staff of Art News _and formerly was managing editor of the_ Art News Annual.

105

On Having My Portrait Painted

By SOMERSET MAUGHAM

One day, somewhere in the thirties, I received a letter from Marie Laurencin in which she said that she would like to paint a portrait of me. I answered that I should be highly flattered, but felt it only right to remind her that I was not a pretty young thing with the black eyes of a gazelle, a rosebud mouth, and a pink and white complexion, but an elderly party with a sallow skin and a lot of wrinkles. To this she replied that that was no matter, but she would like me to come in a dressing gown because she didn't know how to paint a coat. A date was fixed for the first sitting, and because I was too timid to walk through the streets of Paris in a bright blue dressing gown, I carried it over my arm. I sat to Marie Laurencin for four long afternoons during which she told me the story of her life and loves. I have seldom enjoyed myself more. Toward the end of the fourth afternoon she put down her brushes and, leaning back, looked at the canvas on which she had been working. "*Vous savez*," she said, "*on se plaint toujours que mes portraits ne sont pas ressemblants. Je ne peux pas vous dire à quel point je m'en fous.*" That may be translated: "You know people always complain that my portraits aren't likenesses. I must tell you that I don't care a ——." I will leave the reader to add the last word himself. Then she took the canvas off the easel and said: "Here you are. It's a present." I don't think that anyone could suppose that I ever looked like that, but it was a charming gesture on Marie Laurencin's part and I am grateful for it.

I can't believe that the features of any private person have been more often drawn, painted, etched, and sculptured than mine. By private person I mean someone who has not won distinction in politics, war, on the stage, in films, or by exalted station. If posterity should want to know what I looked like it will have ample opportunity, but it may well be that posterity will have more important things to concern itself with.

It all began many years ago. In 1904 I spent a year in Paris. I was then an obscure but promising novelist. I made the acquaintance of a young Irish painter, Gerald Kelly by name, who had a studio on the Left Bank of the Seine. He was a voluble and amusing talker; I am a good listener. We became great friends. It must have been two or three years later, when we were both again living in England, that he asked me to sit to him for a portrait. I had never been asked to do that before and was delighted. I do not know what happened to the portrait Gerald Kelly painted then; it may be that he was not satisfied with it and destroyed it. The years went by. I was no longer a promising but obscure novelist; I was a popular playwright. In 1908 I had four plays running in London at the same time. Gerald Kelly painted a portrait of me which is here illustrated; of all the portraits he has painted of me, this is that which I like best. Later he did another portrait called *The Jester*, which was bought by the Tate Gallery. In all he has painted eleven portraits of me. I need hardly add that in due course he became president of the Royal Academy and painted the state portraits of King George VI and his consort, Queen Elizabeth.

I have an idea that there are two sorts of portrait painters, the painter who is chiefly concerned with his sitter and the painter who is chiefly concerned with himself. The object of the first is to produce an exact likeness of his sitter. Super-

MR. MAUGHAM

Maugham by Laurencin

LADY JOHN HOPE

Maugham's favorite Kelly

THE TATE GALLERY

The Jester by Kelly

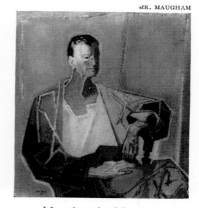

MR. MAUGHAM

Maugham by MacAvoy

cilious critics condemn portraits of this kind as photographic and claim that they have nothing to do with art. For all I know they are right; but what they forget is that with the passage of time, when the sitter's clothes have become costume, so that the picture has become a period piece, it may have a decorative value which is not without charm. The painter of the second sort is not particularly concerned to produce a speaking likeness of his sitter: to satisfy the client, he may take some pains to describe on canvas the impression the sitter has made on him, but his real use, the sitter's use, I mean, is to provide an essential element in the general pattern which will result in a work of art.

I have twice been painted by artists who had some such idea. One is Edouard MacAvoy (a Frenchman despite his Scottish name) and the other is Graham Sutherland. It was late in the thirties that MacAvoy asked me to sit to him. He made elaborate drawings of my head and my hands, but then war broke out and the sittings were suspended. I did not see him again till after peace was declared. He told me then that he had finished the picture and was going to exhibit it in the Autumn Salon. This he did and it created something of a sensation. I have been told that Braque greatly admired it; he is reported to have said: "I have only one criticism to make. The left side of the face is slightly realistic." I own the picture and I find it a very easy one to live with.

It was soon after the war was over that I made the acquaintance of Graham Sutherland. He had rented a house on the Riviera not far from where I live and I met him at various parties. I knew very little about his work, but I had been told that he was talented and I discovered for myself that he had great personal charm. (Oddly enough all the painters and sculptors I have had to do with had it.) I noticed that Sutherland looked at me a good deal, but I paid no particular attention to that, and it was a surprise to me when a friend came to me one day and told me that Graham Sutherland had asked him to inquire whether I would sit to him for a portrait. I gladly consented. He had never painted a portrait before and so this was in the nature of an amusing experiment. His method, again somewhat to my surprise, was the same as Edouard MacAvoy's; he made careful drawings of my head and my hands, which he preferred not to show me, and I saw nothing of the portrait till it was entirely finished. The experiment succeeded, and I think it is no exaggeration when I say that this portrait made Graham Sutherland's fortune. Since then he has painted several excellent portraits, but I do not know that he has ever painted a better one than mine.

Somerset Maugham had been established for many years as an eminent man of letters when he sat for this portrait by Graham Sutherland in 1949. Since then Sutherland has painted Sir Winston Churchill (see page 103) and Lord Beaverbrook, but critics agree with Maugham that Sutherland's portrait of him is the painter's best.

By FRANCIS RUSSELL

ROBERT SHORE

THE WITCH OF BEACON HILL

Boston doctors and Harvard professors ventured into a

lively spirit world with the medium known as Margery

Never in the ambiguous history of spiritualism in the United States has there been a medium who achieved such a world reputation for psychic phenomena and caused such extended controversy as the woman known as Margery, who suddenly manifested her abilities in Boston in the spring of 1923. Margery, it was claimed, performed under the spirit control of her dead brother Walter. His voice first spoke through her, though later independently of her vocal cords. During a series of Margery's séances extraordinary occurrences took place. Flowers and other objects materialized from nowhere. Ghostly bugle calls sounded. At times ectoplasmic rods sprouted from the medium's body that were capable of touching persons in the dark, moving objects, producing lights, and making wax impressions of themselves. J. Malcolm Bird, associate editor of *Scientific American*, who later wrote a book on Margery, became her partisan as did Hereward Carrington, Sir Arthur Conan Doyle, and others. Houdini, the magician who had attended five of the séances, denounced her almost hysterically. In the next few years hundreds of newspaper and magazine articles appeared about her. A committee from *Scientific American* and one from Harvard investigated her, and their findings were varied. Concerning Margery herself there has never been a final conclusion.

What made Margery's case unique beyond the spiritualist phenomena themselves was the quality of the people involved. Doctors, professional men, and members of the Harvard faculty were among the regular sitters at her séances. No financial considerations ever entered into the mediumship; in fact the expenses of many of the investigators were paid by Margery's husband.

Margery was the Canadian-born wife of Le Roi Goddard Crandon, a well-known Boston doctor and surgeon-in-chief of a local hospital. Dr. Crandon, a Harvard graduate of the class of 1894, had been for some years a lecturer in surgery at the Harvard Medical School. The Crandons lived in a four-story Federalist town house at 10 Lime Street, just at the foot of Beacon Hill. It is a small street of dissimilar houses harmonized by the passage of time, and its antique intimacy makes it seem rather fitting for psychic adventures.

The name Margery was a pseudonym invented for Mrs. Crandon at the outset of her mediumship to protect her from publicity. In her ordinary daily life she was matter-of-fact about her psychic powers and would sometimes jokingly refer to herself—a personable woman in her thirties—as a witch, adding that if she had lived 250 years earlier she would probably have been hanged.

Margery the medium had her origins in Dr. Crandon's library. More or less by chance, early in 1923 he happened to take up books on spiritualism, at first in a desultory way and later with more concentrated interest. Although his wife did not take spiritualism seriously they talked about it together, and one day as a joke she went with a friend to a Boston clairvoyant. She did not identify herself, and she was astonished when the medium, in a trance, told her that a spirit by the name of Walter was present. The messages that he then transmitted from Walter consisted of small personal incidents from her girlhood.

A short time after this the Crandons, with four of their friends, made a private attempt at spirit communication, gathering around a table in the Lime Street living room under a red light. Before long the table began to rotate and then tilt. One by one the sitters were sent from the room. Only in Mrs. Crandon's absence did the table remain dead. A code of responses was soon established by which the table-tipping intelligence, who maintained he was Walter, could reply to questions. Subsequently Walter began to communicate by a series of raps, and then after some time his voice asserted itself through Margery. About this time Dr. Crandon constructed a cabinet for his wife, and her séances were conducted with the sitters joining hands in a circle.

Walter's presence was usually announced by a sharp whistle. His voice now became a standard feature of all Margery's séances, and the table tipping and the raps were discarded. Over the months her mediumship seemed to follow its own curious progress. At one point all the clocks in the house were stopped at a time predetermined by Walter. At another séance Walter announced he would play taps, and shortly afterward the notes were faintly heard in the lower part of the house. Sometimes the furniture in the living room would move. Once, after he called attention to the possibility, a live pigeon was found in the next room.

Finally Dr. Crandon claimed that he had observed "faint aurora-like emanations" projecting from the region of Margery's fingers. This was the beginning of the ectoplasmic materializations that were to produce organs and hands of various kinds. A wax cast was made of one of these hands. Others were photographed. Walter registered his thumbprint in wax. The ectoplasmic limbs rang bells. Accompanying these materializations were psychic lights that floated about the room glowing and fading.

In 1922 *Scientific American* offered to pay $2,500 for any objective demonstration of psychic phenomena and appointed an investigating committee of five prominent persons interested in this subject. The members were Dr. Daniel Comstock, formerly professor of physics at the Massachusetts Institute of Technology; Dr. William McDougall, professor of psychology at Harvard and president of the American Society for Psychical Research; Dr. Walter Franklin Prince, former clergyman and research officer of the society; Dr. Hereward Carrington, the author and psychic experimenter who had tested the European medium Palladino; and Harry Houdini, the magician and escape artist. J. Malcolm Bird, who had first brought Margery into contact with the committee, served as its secretary. During 1924, in the course of the committee's investigations, three articles by Mr. Bird essentially favorable to Margery appeared in *Scientific American*. These spread the interest in her mediumship quickly and widely.

The report of the committee a few months later was, however, unfavorable. Mr. Bird accepted the Lime Street séance phenomena as genuine, as did Dr. Carrington. Houdini, with a showman's eye for publicity, published a lurid pamphlet denouncing Margery. Dr. Prince was not convinced. Yet it must be said that his and Houdini's attendance at the sittings was scanty. Dr. Comstock was present more often than any of the others. He found difficulty in making up his mind, and concluded merely that "rigid proof has not yet been furnished." Dr. McDougall also seemed hesitant during the séances, but in his report he wrote: "As long ago as November . . . I was inclined to regard all the phenomena I had observed as produced by normal means. . . . Since that date . . . the inclination has grown steadily stronger in the main, in spite of some minor fluctuations, and has now become well-nigh irresistible." The report and the committee were sharply attacked by the growing number of Margery's defenders.

In the summer of 1925, another briefer investigation was conducted by a group of younger members of the Harvard faculty, this time in a room of Emerson Hall in the Harvard Yard. Walter made the transition from Lime Street easily, but the principal Emerson phenomenon was Margery's trance production "after the manner of a birth" of an ectoplasmic hand. For these séances she wore luminous bands on her legs as controls, but during one sitting it was discovered that she had slipped a foot out of the band and was free to manipulate it. Afterward a committee member, by a similar free use of his foot, managed to duplicate all the phenomena except the production of ectoplasm. The ectoplasmic hand impressed itself on a lump of plasticine, which on later examination showed skin markings and lint microscopically identical with that in the medium's slipper. At another Emerson séance two observers noted that the medium had worked both hands free, and one of them detected her conveying objects from her lap and afterward returning them. Internal examination of the medium was never permitted.

At a subsequent series of séances with an English repre-

sentative of the Society for Psychical Research, Margery produced varieties of ectoplasm including a much more embryonic hand than the earlier one, spongy and feeling like blancmange. This hand was photographed under red light. When these photographs were examined by Dr. W. B. Cannon, professor of physiology, and Dr. H. W. Rand, professor of zoology, both of Harvard, they reported that the so-called ectoplasm was composed of the lung tissue of some animal.

There were rumors that the Harvard group had disagreed about Margery. To correct this the members issued a statement that they were "in absolute agreement that the only conclusion possible is that trickery accounted for all the phenomena; and that the only possible difference of opinion is to what extent the trickery is unconscious."

Perhaps the most directly damaging evidence against Margery was the discovery in 1932 that the wax impressions shown for six years as Walter's psychic thumbprints were really those of a Boston dentist. The dentist, still alive and practicing, admitted that he had once made several such impressions in dental wax at Mrs. Crandon's request. To this charge the Crandons never replied.

A friend of mine who was at that time an English instructor at Harvard attended several of the Lime Street sittings. He had just published his first novel, *River's End*. What he experienced in the séance room at first convinced him, and he gave Margery a copy of his book in which he had written: "I have seen, and I have believed." In the course of further sittings, however, he came to change his opinion and in the end very much regretted that he had given Margery the inscribed book.

"At one séance," he told me, "Margery produced an ectoplasmic hand and we were asked to feel it. As soon as I touched it I knew it was the hand of a dead person. It was small, either a child's or a woman's, but dead. I understood then. Dr. Crandon was a surgeon, and he could sneak such things out of the hospital."

"But," I asked him, "if it was a fraud, why did they do it?"

"It was a weird business," he said. "Crandon was much older than his wife, and he was an educated man of some standing. She had neither education nor background. There may have been some sort of psychological conflict in that, each trying to prove something to the other. Of course he faked, but perhaps he felt that in spite of the trickery there was something real behind it all. He may have believed in Walter. I don't know. After that night I never went near Lime Street again."

It was in 1940, in the second autumn of the war, that I happened to be asked to 10 Lime Street. I was surprised to learn that Margery still lived there. In the ominous quiet of an America preparing its first peacetime draft, the controversy she had caused a decade and a half earlier seemed remote and irrelevant. Yet though the fashions of publicity had passed her by, Margery still continued her sittings with her followers. Dr. Crandon had died the winter before.

A Dr. Richardson introduced me. He had been a friend of the Crandons from the beginning of Margery's mediumship. Just after World War I he lost his two sons in a polio epidemic and this had turned him towards spiritualism. To his satisfaction at least, he had found his boys again in all the brightness of their youth at Margery's séances. On our way to Lime Street he showed me a spirit photograph of Margery in a trance with a cloud like a double exposure above her head on which were the blurred outlines of two faces. These faces, he told me, were his sons beyond doubt.

We arrived at eight o'clock of a rainy, line-storm evening. Margery herself opened the street-level door for us, shook hands, and led the way to an upstairs drawing room. She was an overdressed, dumpy little woman, amiable, yet with a faint elusive coarseness about her that one sensed as soon as she spoke. Dr. Richardson said that in recent séances they had been trying to reach Dr. Crandon and that tonight they hoped to get a wax imprint of his fingers. The room was a homely one with chintz curtains, leather and fabric armchairs, imitation upright Chippendales, a tapestry brick fireplace with a sofa in front of it at one end and lengths of bookcases at the other. On a side shelf was a silver-framed photograph signed A. Conan Doyle, and another of Sir Oliver Lodge. Near the window stood an old-fashioned Victrola. There were eight or ten people standing about.

"Everybody ready?" Margery asked us. We arranged our chairs in a circle. Margery sat in the center in a straight-backed chair. "Let's have a little music," she said as we settled down.

Someone turned on the Victrola. She squatted there with her eyes half-closed, and there was no sound but the rasp of the needle and then the notes of "Ah Sweet Mystery of Life" scratched out of the wax grooves.

The song ended, and as the mechanism shut itself off, Dr. Richardson turned out the lights. For several minutes there was no sound at all. The tension hung suspended like that empty moment before the bull comes into the arena. Then I noticed Margery's breathing. At first it sounded no more than a repeated sigh, but with each breath she took it deepened until it became a stertorous moan. Only once before had I heard such sounds—when I passed a hospital room where a man was dying.

Then, breaking in suddenly over this animal noise that stopped abruptly, came a rush of air and an ear-cracking whistle, and after this a man's voice talking very fast. The sound seemed to come from a spot several feet above Margery's head.

"Almost thought I couldn't make it," said the voice nasally. "Lot of interrupters, lots of trouble, plenty of them."

Dr. Richardson spoke back. "Walter," he said, "we have a new sitter with us I'd like you to meet. This is Mr. Russell."

"How do you do," I said awkwardly in what I thought was his general direction, realizing as I said it that my voice sounded strained and somewhat artificial.

"How do *you* do," said Walter mimicking me. "I don't think you do very well. Is that a Harvard accent you have?"

"You mustn't mind Walter," said Dr. Richardson. "He's often rude, but he doesn't really mean a thing by it."

"That's what the doc thinks," said Walter.

A woman in the darkness opposite asked if Dr. Crandon could give them any message.

"Roy's busy," Walter answered her. "He said to say he was O.K., but he's still tied up. He can't come through yet."

"When do you think he can?" Mrs. Richardson asked.

"Not for awhile yet, not for awhile yet. Keep your shirt on." Walter's voice was edged. "Leave him alone, give him time. He's got his troubles too."

There was more talk, and then Dr. Richardson asked Walter about the fingerprints.

"Not tonight, Doc," said Walter. "Next time, maybe."

Then there was silence, as if a radio station had gone off the air, and a few seconds later Margery's voice broke in casually. "Will you turn on the lights?" Although pitched in another key, the tone bore a certain resemblance to Walter's.

The lights went on and we stood up blinking, while Margery smiled at us in an indolent good-natured way, stretching her plump arms and yawning. As we left she shook hands with each of us at the top of the landing. "You must all come to tea next Sunday," she said. "I have a feeling it's going to be important. All of you, next Sunday—but not before five o'clock. I have to see about Roy's grave earlier." She giggled. "The landscape gardeners have made an awful mess of it, planted hydrangeas. Roy hates hydrangeas. Now don't forget—next Sunday at five."

It was the only time I ever saw Margery. At that séance there had been no wandering lights or ghostly music, no bells ringing, no psychic touches I could feel, no ectoplasm or even fingerprints. In a committee sense there had not been enough phenomena for anyone to pass judgment; yet Walter's voice was real, and he was the core of the matter,

the leading spirit—if one could excuse the play on words. Those earlier productions of ectoplasm had been a contrivance, part of the paraphernalia that Dr. Crandon had assembled. A less gullible medical man than Dr. Richardson was afterward to describe the psychic rods sprouting from Margery's body as some sort of animal intestines stuffed with cotton. The lights and the bells and the rest, Houdini could have managed as well.

That left Walter, a spirit with a taste for Victor Herbert, brash and crude of speech, a kind of poolroom johnny from the other world. As an audible actuality he was capable of three interpretations. Either he was a disembodied entity that had once been Margery's brother; or he was a subconscious element of Margery's developed in a trance; or he was merely Margery's normal self play-acting.

If one were to believe the first interpretation, as did Dr. Richardson, that glimpsed other world must be a shabby, static place. For Walter, since parting from his body, showed no development in mind or personality or tastes.

In regard to the latter two interpretations, the first seems the more likely. For Margery to contrive such a conscious Walter-fiction during hundreds of sittings over a period of years would be too demanding a feat. Walter was a complete individual. He never hesitated, never lacked for words, never stepped out of character. Rather than to assume that Margery was merely a clever actress, it seems a more likely assumption that her trances at least were genuine and that Walter was a second personality developed in them.

Three years after that Lime Street séance, when I had been sent overseas to an infantry reinforcement unit in England, I happened to pick up a 1942 copy of an English almanac in the mess anteroom. While I waited for dinner, I thumbed through it—the events of the year before, tides, eclipses, weights and measures, and finally a list of noted people who had died during the year. There under November's obituaries I suddenly noticed: "Mrs. L. R. G. Crandon, the medium Margery, at Boston, Massachusetts, U.S.A."

It was not quite, however, my last contact with Margery. One heat-struck August afternoon just after the war, I happened to be walking along Cornhill behind Boston's city hall. As a relief to that empty, sun-bleached street I stopped under the shadow of the awning in front of Colesworthy's secondhand bookstore. On the sidewalk was the usual tray of twenty-five-cent books. As I glanced over them I saw one with a faded brown cover that looked familiar. I could scarcely decipher the lettering of the title, *River's End*. I picked it up and opened it. There on the flyleaf, just as I had somehow expected, was the neat, almost prim inscription: "I have seen, and I have believed."

Francis Russell is the author of many magazine articles and Three Studies in Twentieth-Century Obscurity. *He wrote the article "Frost in the Evening" for the November issue of* HORIZON.

L'EMPRUNT DE LA LIBÉRATION

On the eve of victory the French raise a Liberation Loan to speed the Kaiser's doom.

EUROPE IN ANGUISH

A collection of posters preserved from the First World War's aftermath
recalls great propaganda art and the desperate years that produced it

The harsh but compelling documents reproduced on the following eight pages are a selection of political posters that were thrown upon the walls and billboards of five European countries during the turbulent, explosive years 1918-22. They are all, in a word, propaganda. But they are also a vivid form of pictorial shorthand for recording the history of a tragic era.

Because they were designed to stop a man in his tracks, their meaning is unmistakable in almost any language. One has only to glance at them to know what they are about: war, aftermath of war, hunger, unemployment, age-old resentments, brand-new remedies, ephemeral hopes, and lingering despair. In short, they reflect all the ambiguous promises and defeated illusions of the time that liquidated the First World War and laid the foundation for the Second.

We in America are familiar with the story but not with this method of telling it, for posters like these are peculiarly European. Such mordant images have seldom accosted the passer-by in an American street. This is good for our political stability, but it makes a harder task for the historian.

No one leafing through a collection of contemporary American posters, with their suave reminders that a whiskey is known by the company it keeps, could learn very much about the political ideas and impulses that accompanied us through the first half of the twentieth century.

It is otherwise in Europe, where every shifting allegiance and emerging emotion has been recorded with searing precision on vacant walls and kiosks from Moscow to Vienna and Paris. Recorded, but not preserved. For the poster is a fragile and transient art, committed to perishable materials. It is the prey of rain, wind, sun, and eventual indifference. Only a few scattered efforts have been made to preserve its works—many of them of artistic as well as historic value. One of the most impressive undertakings in this respect is the collection amassed by Levi Berman in New York, from

TEXT CONTINUED ON PAGE 121

On the devastated land, at war's end, a songbird heralds a new day of peace. This poster was drawn by Steinlen (a name in French poster art second only to Toulouse-Lautrec) to raise money for the Liberated Provinces: "Let your aid to our unhappy brothers be generous!"

112

JOURNÉE DES RÉGIONS LIBÉRÉES

QUE VOTRE AIDE À NOS FRÈRES MALHEUREUX SOIT GÉNÉREUSE!

ЦАРЬ, ПОП И БОГАЧ

НА ПЛЕЧАХ У ТРУДОВОГО НАРОДА.

Три владыки, три господина мира едут на плечах рабочих и крестьян по тощей, разоренной земле, по трупам и костям погибших бедняков.

Эти три владыки—царь, поп и жадный, ненасытный богач-капиталист.

В руках у капиталиста—бич, на боку у него висит меч, покрытый кровью. Бичом он хлещет рабочий народ, заставляет тащить проклятую ношу. Мечом он гонит народ на войну, на бойню. Пускай бедняки завоюют ему в чужих странах новые земли и богатства.

Так было раньше в России. Теперь рабочие и крестьяне сбросили жадных кровопийц. Но во Франции, Англии, Америке короли, попы и богачи еще уцелели. Они гонят теперь свои полки на Россию, хотят помочь царскому отродью, попам, кулакам снова сесть на шею русского народа.

Рабочие и крестьяне! Хотите ли вы опять проливать для грабителей пот и кровь? Хотите ли жить в голоде и холоде и отдавать бездельникам все свои богатства? Хотите ли опять катать на своих плечах царя, попов, помещиков, богачей?

Если не хотите, отбивайте поход иностранных королей и богачей. Помогайте Советской власти, давайте побольше хлеба, работы, солдат в Красную Армию! Подымайтесь все защищать свою власть, землю и волю!

ВТОРАЯ ГОСУДАРСТВЕННАЯ ТИПОГРАФИЯ.
Москва. Трехпрудный пер., 9.

Издательство Всероссийского Центрального Исполнит. Комитета Советов Рабочих, Крестьянск., Красноарм. и Казачьих Депутатов.

A new conflagration overtakes the old: in Europe's East, war turns into revolution. On the facing page, a Bolshevik poster assails the triumvirate of "Czar, Priest and Rich Man" who "ride on the shoulders of the workers and peasants, over a destroyed earth, over the corpses and bones of the dead poor." Chief of the oppressors is the capitalist: "With his whip he drives the working people . . . with his sword he drives people to war." Acclaiming the overthrow achieved in Russia's October Revolution, the poster warns that "in France, England and America the kings, the priests and the rich still rule" and are sending forces to put down the Russian people's revolt. So, "Rise all, to defend your power, your land, your will!"

At right, over the name of War Commissar Leon Trotsky, the Red Army exhorts its men to "BE ON GUARD!" against Polish interventionists who are trying to "stir up war" under the leadership of Pilsudski, behind whom stand "the biggest French imperialists" (denoted by an aged figure in Gallic uniform). But the Soviet legions once again will destroy the bands of Polish adventurers; "The Red Army will do its work and nothing will stop it."

Below, the Red tide sweeping across Europe is welcomed in splintered, postwar Austria in an election poster. Evidently it did not occur to the artist that his image of a blood-red wave threatening to engulf everything in its path might provoke a response opposite from the one he had intended. Shear off its "Vote Communist" slogan, and it could be read as a message against the insurgents.

Nieder mit dem Bolschewismus
Bolschewismus bringt Krieg und Verderben, Hunger und Tod.
Vereinigung zur Bekämpfung des Bolschewismus. Berlin W. 9. Schellingstr. 2

Above, a major German artist enlists in the combat: "Down with Bolshevism; Bolshevism brings war and ruin, hunger and death" is the message of the expressionist Oskar Kokoschka. Below, the Rhenish city of Essen remembers its dead and asks aid for those bearing the burdens of occupation.

Deutsche Männer schützt Eure Heimat
Tretet ein beim
STURMBATAILLON SCHMIDT
der Garde Kavallerie-Schützen-Division
Infanteristen (Sturmsoldaten) Kavalleristen (Pferdepfleger u. Fahrer)
M.G.Scharfschützen, Minenwerfer, Flammenwerfer, Panzerkraftwagen,
Tanksoldaten, Artilleristen, Handwerker, Monteure u. s w.
ANNAHME STELLE
Berlin·Charlottenburg, Nürnbergerstr. 63

Beaten by the West and undermined by revolution from the East, Central Europe became a seething battleground of rival extremists. Above, in the midst of Germany's military and social breakdown, a poster recruits veterans for one of the many mercenary private armies that sprang up like vigilante bands to keep self-appointed order and prey upon leftist opponents. Here the "Storm Battalion Schmidt" calls for infantrymen, cavalrymen, machine-gun sharpshooters, flame-throwers, tankers, artillerymen, etc. Such freebooting formations of German condottieri eventually fed manpower into the revival of the Reich's military strength.

On the facing page, an apocalyptic revolutionary figure is shown putting the torch to the guardian of such liberties as postwar Austrians possessed—the Parliament at Vienna. Yet this placard, which caused a sensation when slapped upon the Danubian capital's billboards in 1920, does not preach resistance to the incendiaries at all, but the reverse. "Vote Communist!" is its message. Such rabid incitement to violence served to foment further incitements on the opposite side, until the battle of the posters led to physical battles in the streets.

Vergeßt uns nicht!

Opferwoche Essen
3. bis 10. Mai.

SO HABE ICH DAS CHRISTENTUM NICHT GEMEINT!

Turmoil along the Danube: above, Christ's image is used to assail priests; below, city dwellers are shown as victims of peasant greed.

DENKET AN DAS GETREIDEGESTZ und EUREN HUNGER!

KEINE STIMME DEN BROTVERTEUERERN! WÄHLET SOZIALDEMOKRATISCH

In the face of Nazi and militarist revival in Central Europe, pacifist groups in victorious but stricken Britain cry out against any further war. Below, an ex-enemy reaction to British drives for European stability: a "hate" poster laying blame for industrial unemployment at Britain's doorstep.

While a repulsed Christ in Austria (opposite) is represented as saying, "This isn't what I meant by Christianity," and blind struggles break out between city and country folk, a new tribe of sleek and self-important manipulators emerges, claiming to have all the answers: the Nazis. The poster above, a classic in European political art, is one of the earliest efforts of anti-Nazis to satirize the new would-be harbingers of Teutonic destiny. Both men, the fat and the lean, wear along with swastika insignia the headgear of German university dueling fraternities—source of much of the new demagoguery. "Do you want these to rule you?" asks the text; "if not, then vote Social Democratic."

which these posters are taken.

The era covered by these posters opens with the carefully marshaled patriotism that had sustained the Allied nations through the end of the exhausting war. The war's progress had been glacial in its slowness; patience was running out. But one more appeal was made for unity, for dedication, and above all for funds. "Liberation" still meant emancipation from the Kaiser's hosts, though Wilson had altered the definition. To him it meant not only liberation *from* but liberty *to be* on your own, even if this meant proclaiming new national identities irrespective of the past.

But for the moment the ideas seemed to work. The Allies were still allied, except for the defection of Russia. The vaulting aspirations of Imperial Germany had led her into the trap that history sets for the overambitious; facing defeat, her government crumbled in revolution. The decayed façade of the Austro-Hungarian monarchy came down with a crash. And the victors thought they were looking into the dawn of a new millennium. It was in this dawn that Steinlen drew the songbird of peace on page 113.

But a spoiling cloud had already appeared in the east, above Russia. Revolution there had not only overthrown the Czarists but had torn apart the fabric of society. Bolshevism was the new threat, total upheaval the new prospect. In November, 1918, in Germany, workers' and soldiers' councils were set up on the Russian model; the Spartacists were ready to proclaim a German soviet republic. They were stopped just short of success when the Social Democrats withdrew from this uneasy alliance and put them down.

The same story was repeated, with Magyar variations, in Hungary. The largest fragment of the old Hapsburg empire, it had also proclaimed itself a republic in 1918. In the following year the Social Democrats agreed to fuse with the Communists and establish a dictatorship of the proletariat in alliance with Soviet Russia. This produced the shattering five-month regime of Béla Kun. Then the rightists took over, Béla Kun fled to Vienna to be interned in an insane asylum, the White Terror outdid even the Red Terror, and Hungary fossilized into a monarchy without a king.

In fragmented Austria, the Social Democrats decided to pursue their dream alone. Frightened by what had happened

---

AFTERMATH AND PROSPECT

The curtain falls upon the long front in France and Flanders. The soothing hands of Time and Nature, the swift repair of peaceful industry, have already almost effaced the crater fields and the battle lines which in a broad belt from the Vosges to the sea lately blackened the smiling fields of France. . . . Merciful oblivion draws its veils; the crippled limp away; the mourners fall back into the sad twilight of memory. . . .

Is this the end? Is it to be merely a chapter in a cruel and senseless story? Will a new generation in their turn be immolated to square the black accounts of Teuton and Gaul? Will our children bleed and gasp again in devastated lands? Or will there spring from the very fires of conflict that reconciliation of the three giant combatants, which would unite their genius and secure to each in safety and freedom a share in rebuilding the glory of Europe?

Winston S. Churchill, closing passage of his war memoirs, *The World Crisis, 1916-1918*

---

in Hungary, they rejected alliance with the Communists, beat them at the polls, and kept alive the fugitive illusion of democracy until 1934. But even as the Red threat subsided, Austria became the microcosmic battleground of every force that wracked Europe between World Wars I and II. Its capital was socialist and industrial "Red Vienna"; its hinterland was conservative, religious, and agricultural. These opposites were never resolved; the nation was left in a treacherous equilibrium between Right and Left, clericalism and anticlericalism, farmer and worker.

Postwar inflation ran its dizzy course through Central Europe, leaving whole classes pauperized and resentful. The Germans, who had never recognized the inevitability of their defeat, chafed at the occupation of the Ruhr and the restrictions of the Versailles Treaty. They felt old martial stirrings, and began secretly to rearm.

The nations that had supposedly won the war averted their eyes from this unnerving spectacle and wrapped themselves in their own concerns. French cabinets began to practice the tumbling act that they were to bring to futile perfection in the 1930's and again under the Fourth Republic. Britain remained stable enough politically, but she was jarred by bruising strikes and weakened by loss of blood. The United States, insulated by the Atlantic, was busy buying a ticket to Utopia at the stockbroker's.

Men of good will everywhere reaffirmed their devotion to peace and, sometimes, worked to preserve it. Frock-coated diplomats scurried from one green-draped conference table to another, stitching up pacts and treaties with their fountain pens; a tuck here, a patch there, and maybe the fabric would hold. It held, as we know, for another ten years or so. But already by 1922 the Nazis had emerged in Germany— a corporal's guard of bully-boys, malcontents, and sullen leftovers from the Kaiser's army. Even their firmest opponents, the Social Democrats, sometimes seemed to regard them as merely oafish. And already in 1922 Mussolini, farther south, was preparing a new "heroic age" for the Italians.

These years need not have turned out the way they did. Nothing was inevitable—not even a World War II. But, looking at the testimony of these posters, it almost seems to have been so.

Peace, peace, where there is no peace: the International Labor Syndicate calls for "War against War."

Space and the Spirit of Man

CONTINUED FROM PAGE 30

Archbishop Ussher's date for Genesis—4004 B.C.—which may still be found in some Bibles. It is indeed curious that so many devout men, during the three hundred years between Galileo and Darwin, stubbornly refused to recognize the grandeur of the universe in space and time—almost as if determined to disparage the power of God. The Eastern religions avoided this mistake, which has done so much to weaken the prestige of Christianity.

As mankind's modest place in the scheme of the universe is more and more widely recognized—on the emotional as well as the intellectual level—the effects on our racial pride will certainly be profound. To the Psalmist's question, "What is Man, that Thou art mindful of him?" the Future may well give the ironic answer "What, indeed?" Our species has come into existence in the last five-thousandth of the Earth's history, and the entire span of human civilization extends over barely a millionth of that time. Unless we exhibit a conceit which can be aptly termed astronomical, we must assume that there are many, many species in the universe far more advanced than ours, intellectually as well as spiritually. Indeed, the extreme youth of Homo sapiens on any cosmic time scale makes it likely that the vast majority of rational extraterrestrial creatures must be superior to us by millions of years of development.

This prospect has been viewed with some alarm by many Christians who find it hard to reconcile the existence of other intelligent species with the doctrines of Incarnation and Redemption. If God made man in His own image, what of all the other creatures who must be made in different images, if they are to survive on alien worlds? And if Christ has saved us alone, what have *we* done to merit such special treatment?

During the last few years these problems—which once seemed quite as abstract as the classic question of the number of angels who could dance on a pin—have engaged several theologians. In his *Systematic Theology*, Professor Paul Tillich points out that the Incarnation preached by Christianity is for mankind only but that other life may have other incarnations—an idea expressed in another way by Alice Meynell in her poem "Christ in the Universe":

> . . . in the eternities,
> Doubtless we shall compare together, hear
> A million alien Gospels, in what guise
> He trod the Pleiades, the Lyre, the Bear.

Tillich goes on to conclude: "The manifestation of saving power in one place implies that saving power is operating in all places. The expectation of the Messiah as the bearer of the New Being presupposes that 'God loves the universe,' even though in the appearance of the Christ he actualizes this love for historical man alone."

Undoubtedly the most stimulating writer on these matters is C. S. Lewis, professor of literature at Magdalen College, Cambridge, and author of the famous *Screwtape Letters*. In two novels, *Out of the Silent Planet* and *Perelandra*, Lewis has developed the theme that only humanity has fallen, and that the creatures on other planets are free of the guilt that requires our redemption. This view of mankind's peculiar depravity, well justified by a glance at the daily papers, implies that our planet is under quarantine; and in a recent issue of the *Christian Herald* Professor Lewis makes it clear that he regards with some disfavor our current attempts to escape this quarantine.

Another possibility, but one so flattering to our pride that it is hard to believe it can be true, is that the redemption of other races will proceed through us—that man, in fact, may one day take salvation to the stars. Remembering how "gun and gospel" have been combined in the past, and the manner in which so many missionaries have attempted to "civilize the natives," Lewis is not at all happy about this prospect. "Would all our missionaries," he asks, "recognize an unfallen race if they met it? Would they continue to press upon creatures that did not need to be saved that plan of Salvation which God has appointed for Man? Would they denounce as sins mere differences of behavior which the spiritual and biological history of these strange creatures fully justified?" Anyone who has read accounts of past mission activities (Bradford Smith's *Yankees in Paradise* is an excellent example) will appreciate the force of these questions, and Lewis argues nobly: "You and I should resolve to stand firm against all exploitation and all theological imperialism . . . Our loyalty is due not to our species but to God. Those who are, or can become His sons, are our real brothers even if they have shells or tusks. It is spiritual, not biological kinship that counts."

The Roman Catholic Church has already accepted and welcomed the coming of the space age. (Perhaps the out-

The eleventh-century Bayeux Tapestry indicates the awe with which a comet, considered as an evil omen, was regarded.

standing role that Jesuit scientists have played in astrophysics has something to do with this.) In 1956 the International Astronautical Federation held a congress in Rome and heard an address from the Pope in which he expressed the view that, now that man has discovered the means of exploring the universe, God clearly intends him to use it. This is a teaching which most men, whatever their beliefs, will surely accept. Any path to knowledge is a path to God—or to Reality, whichever word one prefers to use.

We may conclude, therefore, that any fears that space exploration will shatter the bases of existing religions are unfounded. Nevertheless, the tremendous flood of new knowledge that will accrue from space travel (and which indeed is already flowing down from today's satellites) will in due course profoundly modify our philosophical and religious beliefs. Anyone who doubts this, need only glance at the overwhelming impact of science upon faith during the past few centuries; the now settled controversies over the Earth's movement around the sun and the evolution of man are the classic examples. Even in the last hundred years, many beliefs passionately held by the leaders of the great religions have ceased to be accepted by their equally devout successors. It would be absurd to imagine that this process will come to an end just at the moment when science is about to make the greatest breakthrough in all history.

At this moment in time, at the very beginning of the centuries-long gold rush into ever richer, ever expanding fields of knowledge, we must realize that there is no hope of understanding our universe until we have examined a fairly large sample of it—certainly a good deal more than one small planet out of billions. Though this cautious attitude may disappoint many who are hot for certainties, any other policy would be utterly naïve. It would put us in the same position as Pacific islanders who have never yet had any contact with the world beyond their coral reef, yet who attempt to construct a picture of the whole Earth and its peoples from the view from their highest palm tree.

In *Of Stars and Men*, Harlow Shapley writes of our present "anthropocentric religions and philosophies, which have so often been conspicuously earth-bound and much tangled up with the human mind and human behavior," and looks forward to their expanding to embrace these new revelations of science. "A one-planet deity has for me little appeal," he adds. On the other hand, the British astronomer Fred Hoyle, in the controversial series of radio talks that became the well-known book *The Nature of the Universe*, took an uncompromisingly materialist view. He concluded that there is no evidence for the existence of God in the universe around us, religion presumably being an illusion of the human mind.

On the latter view, it must be assumed that when we make contact with superior extraterrestrial intelligences we shall find that belief in a supernatural order of things marks an early stage of development amongst most rational crea-

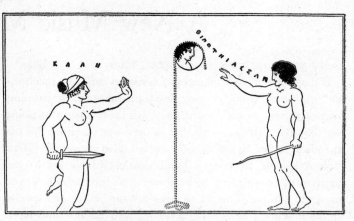

A Greek version of the moon's rise shows it, on a starry chain, being summoned by two magically endowed females.

tures and perishes with the rise of science. Most disconcerting of all would be the discovery that man alone is a myth-making animal, forever impelled to fill the gaps in his knowledge by fantasies. (Yet if this be the price we have had to pay for the whole realm of art, which is always an attempt to create the nonexistent, we need not be ashamed. We will be better off than beings who possess all knowledge but know nothing of poetry and music.)

Whatever the outcome of our discoveries and adventures in space, the fact will remain that the real universe is more miraculous than any miracle. And even if every man now alive seen from a century hence appears no more than "a Pagan suckled in a creed outworn," that will leave God precisely where He has always been, if He is anywhere—back at the beginning of creation, x billion years ago. (As of today, $x = 5$. But remember Archbishop Ussher.) Perhaps when God reached zero of the cosmic countdown, He turned His attention elsewhere, knowing that His work with us was done. It will certainly not diminish His glory—rather the reverse—if we discover that, in all the ages since time began, He has never tinkered with the mechanism of the universe. Only an unskilled craftsman is forced to make perpetual adjustments to his handiwork; the real expert packs his tools and walks away when the job is done.

Let us, therefore, wait in a spirit of expectant humility for whatever light the future may throw upon these great questions, remembering that our intellectual sincerity may well be judged by our lack of apprehension. No honest man was ever afraid of the truth.

Faiths come and go, but Truth abides. Out there among the stars lie such truths as we may understand, whether we learn them by our own efforts, or from the strange teachers who are waiting for us along the infinite road on which our feet are now irrevocably set.

Arthur C. Clarke is a British novelist and science writer who has done extensive work on the exploration of space. His most recent books are Going into Space *and* Earthlight, *both fiction.*

A New Music Made with a Machine

CONTINUED FROM PAGE 54

used by the tape recorder composer himself.

If the modern electronic composer is accused of a mechanical approach when he slows down his material by running his instrument at half speed, then we must hasten to point out that Bach does exactly the same thing when he has his melodies played in longer note values, also giving the effect of half speed. In conventional music, this is known as augmentation—a term well known to anyone who has ever analyzed a fugue. Then, if the modern tape composer speeds up his machine, he is using a device that Bach would have called diminution—the playing of the melody in smaller note values, making for an effect of greater speed.

Should we accuse the electronic composer of lack of soul when he cuts out a portion of his tape and reproduces it repeatedly, in different ways? Then we must level the same accusation against Beethoven, since there is hardly a single extended work by him in which he does not take snippets of his themes and repeat them.

Again, is it a heartless thing to turn a melody upside down on tapes? If so, we must also deny the beauty of a section of the slow movement of Beethoven's String Quartet, Opus 95, where the melody is played alternately upside down and right side up in a technique known to musicians as inversion.

All this is to point out that the methods used by the tapesichord composer are not necessarily a denial of the conventional ways of treating musical ideas. The mere fact that conventional music itself allows such treatment of its ideas may come as something of a disappointment to the more romantic-minded listener, who might be under the impression that a musical composition is nothing more than an unbridled outpouring of emotions, generated by the heat of inspiration. Such listeners might well be reminded that some of the most exciting and emotional portions of Beethoven's symphonies occur in those sections that are called developments, or by the even less glamorous term "working-out sections." Part of the greatness of a composition lies in the manner in which its composer treats—or manipulates—his themes. The tapesichord composer, as he cuts,

re-records, slows down, speeds up, combines, or alters his musical material, is doing nothing that, in principle, cannot be found in the overwhelming majority of the world's compositions in the realm of Western music.

But the mere fact that a composer working with electronic means uses the same aesthetic methods as did his predecessors is no guarantee in itself that his results are going to make good music. Think of how many compositions there are in the conventional idiom that are less than inspiring, despite the fact that their creators knew all the rules. In electronic music no less than in conventional music, the results will depend upon the imagination the composer can bring to bear on his material.

It is in the matter of his basic material—the sounds themselves—that the tapesichord composer finds himself faced with untold possibilities. The basic sounds used by Beethoven, for instance, are quite limited and rather rigidly controlled. Beethoven's music uses only those pitches that can be played on the keys of a piano. But this, in itself, is a completely arbitrary and mechanical restriction that Western music has placed upon itself. It eliminates all the pitches that exist *between* the adjacent notes on the piano. Yet these pitches, or notes, actually do exist, and they are recognized in other systems of music, such as the East Indian.

Then, also, in the matter of *colors* of sounds, Beethoven's music (and, with it, all traditional music) is quite circumscribed. Until the twentieth century, the palette of musical sounds was confined to the human voice, to keyboard instruments such as the clavichord, virginal, harpsichord, piano, and organ, and to the orchestra. This last-named category includes families of instruments that are played by only three methods, which can be humorously described as scraping (the strings), blowing (the wood winds and brass winds), and banging (the percussions). Add those instruments in which the sounds are produced by plucking (the harp, lute, guitar, mandolin, banjo, etc.), and we have the entire gamut of sounds upon which our conventional Western music is based.

That there has always been

TOWARD A MUSIC THAT WILL REALLY SING

The old masters could sing but lacked the teachings of science to supplement those of art—a noble union, which enables moving melody and powerful harmony to be at one. . . . What might we not accomplish if we discovered the physical laws in virtue of which—mark this well—we bring together in proportions as yet unknown the ethereal substance in the air and thereby not only produce music but also perceive the phenomena of light, vegetation, and life itself! Don't you see! Those laws would equip the composer with new powers by making possible instruments far superior to those we have, and perhaps result in a grander harmony than that which governs our present music. . . . Composers have so far worked with a substance they did not understand.

Honoré de Balzac, GAMBARA, translated by Jacques Barzun (in PLEASURES OF MUSIC, edited by Jacques Barzun, Viking Press, 1951).

a desire on the part of composers to extend this range is proven by the very existence of the art of orchestration, and by the increasing emphasis that has been placed on it over the centuries. When Claudio Monteverdi, in the score of his *Il Combattimento di Tancredi e Clorinda*, in 1624 directed his string players to "leave the bow and pinch the strings between two fingers," he created the first pizzicato, thus extending the variety of sounds that had met the ear. In principle, this was no different from the transformations to which the present day tape recorder composer subjects his sounds. In the same work Monteverdi included a passage in which the strings repeated the same note very rapidly. This was the first use of the tremolo, which has since served to heighten the emotional effect of countless orchestral works, operas, movies, and radio and television dramas. In principle, again, this is identical with the rapid repetitions of notes that we so often find in music for tape recorder.

Beethoven, in the scherzo of his String Quartet, Opus 131, directed each of the four players to apply the bow near the bridge of his instrument, thus producing a weird, almost otherworldy effect, oddly suggestive of today's tape recorder music. During the second half of the nineteenth century, Richard Strauss, in his *Don Quixote*, created what is known as "flutter-tonguing" by directing the flutist to roll his tongue in a sound like "d-r-r-r" while playing. Béla Bartók, in his String Quartet No. 6, composed in 1939, had the players slide their fingers along the strings to create an unusual effect. These are just a few of the countless attempts made by composers throughout the last three and a half centuries to extend the range of the sounds used in music.

We now grant that there are pitches that fall between the arbitrarily chosen adjacent notes on the piano. Similarly, is it not possible that there are types of sounds that fall somewhere between the equally arbitrarily chosen ones that are produced by scraping, blowing, banging, or plucking? What justification have we for eliminating from music sounds that are produced by methods other than these four—assuming that they can be found and can be manipulated for musical purposes?

In a manner of speaking, the composer throughout history has attempted to explore those regions. He did so by the only route available to him—the mixing of tones produced by the conventional methods. To be sure, because of the kinds of instruments that were at his disposal, he was still limited to the four standard means, so that in reality he never progressed beyond the barriers imposed by them. But his attempts resulted in the development of some magnificent tonal combinations. By the middle of the nineteenth century, the expanding art of orchestration progressed so far that color assumed an importance in music that it had never had before; it became almost an end in itself.

That can be made clear by a comparison of Mozart's G

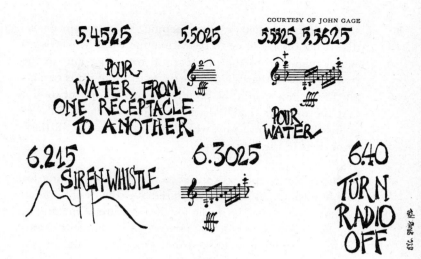

This engaging notation from John Cage's Water Music *suggests the lengths to which some composers go both in music and print.*

Minor Symphony with Ravel's *Daphnis et Chloé* ballet music. If the Mozart symphony were to be played on the piano, where all the instrumental color is reduced to that of the single keyboard instrument, we would still be able to realize the greater part of Mozart's intentions—while denied, of course, the sensuous pleasures imparted by the orchestra. Since the emphasis is on the *musical ideas*—the melodies, or motives, and what happens to them—their development can be followed on the piano. The orchestration, while it enhances the sensuous and emotional aspects of the music, is not indispensable to the development of the ideas.

Ravel's *Daphnis et Chloé* on the other hand places great emphasis upon the sheer sounds of the orchestral instruments. It is less concerned with the intellectual development of thematic ideas than it is with delighting our senses and with creating moods. Played on the piano, the music would lose a great part of its interest because it would emerge monochromatically, like a black-and-white reproduction of a full-color painting. So interested is Ravel in the color aspect of the music, that he even employs human voices, singing without words.

Here we see, then, the trend that music has taken in matters relating to sheer sound. But it is only in the twentieth century, when electronics have made possible the creation and manipulation of sounds other than those produced by the four conventional means, that the composer has been able to make any inroads into other realms. Thus, the new sounds made available by the tape recorder are in reality not a completely new departure but, from a large viewpoint, only an extension of the means at the composer's disposal.

There is very little likelihood that tape recorder music is going to replace music produced in the more conventional manner. It is easy to jump to extreme conclusions and to envisage a world in which automation is so complete that all music is supplied by the machine. To a certain extent that situation *has* come to pass. Imagine what Mozart's reaction might be to the phonograph recording and to the recorded music that is either piped in to restaurants or supplied by a jukebox on the premises. It would appear to him that the machine had indeed taken over. Yet the fact remains that live musicians were necessary to make all these recordings in the first place.

One of the purposes of music is to supply something for people to play. As long as there remains the desire among human beings to make music for the pleasure of making it, whether it be playing for one's self, or in an amateur chamber music group, or an orchestra, or singing in a chorus, the more traditional music will be kept alive. Obviously, listening to a recording, while it can be an important adjunct to our musical life, can never replace the special thrills that come from the actual making of music.

Something roughly analogous holds for the person who does not participate in the performance of music, but who is a listener. It is from these quarters that we may find the greatest resistance to the concept of tape recorder music. The pleasures obtained in the concert hall do not stem solely from the music. There are many peripheral factors that, while they do not pertain immediately to the music itself, nevertheless make concert-going the phenomenon that it is. There is the fact that a concert is a social occasion with all its implications in terms of human relationships. There is the pleasure to be derived from watching a virtuoso in the act of performing. For the serious music student, this may be an important adjunct to his training; for the average listener, it adds to the glamour of the occasion. There is also the fact that the bodily motions of the virtuoso performer or the conductor and the facial expressions of the singer can add materially to our response to the music. Even the very possibility of error cannot be overlooked as a source of excitement.

More important is the fact that live performances always permit varying interpretations of a musical work. The temperaments of different performers bring out different facets of a composition so that the work can be seen in new lights. Even the same performer can take varying approaches to a work, depending upon the conditions of the moment. The special exhilaration that comes to a performer at the moment at which he is revealing a musical work to an audience comes, of course, only from direct contact with the audience. At those moments the presence of the audience "in person" is indispensable to the artist, just as the audience requires the direct association with the performer.

Obviously, tape recorder music eliminates all of the excitements that come from live performances before an audience. Yet, there is another side to the coin. If communication is one of the purposes of music, isn't there as much (or perhaps even more) to be said for communication direct-ly between a *composer* and his audience as for that between a performer and his audience? Is a composer's creation, which is so often the result of much labor, to be used merely as a vehicle for the display of a performer's talents? Moreover, if a composer can find a means of presenting his creation directly to the listener—as *he* conceives it—might that not be preferable to placing his work at the mercy of an interpreter, whose insight might be limited?

Throughout history the composer has been at something of a disadvantage in that he has had no assurance that his brain children would be presented to the world as he conceived them. The dependence upon the interpretations of others, complicated by the fact that our system of writing music is notoriously inexact, has given the composer many occasions for concern. Now at last he is in the position of the painter and sculptor, in that he can present his works as "finished products," without the ministrations of a middleman. Through taped, electronic means he can communicate directly with the audience.

The implications for the music world are rather extensive. For one thing, the need for performing musicians for much new work will be eliminated. A composer need no longer be limited to smaller conceptions merely because he lacks the money to engage large groups of players. Sounds of all volumes will be available to him merely by the turning of a dial. The need for printed music—and, therefore, music publishers—will also disappear. Once the work has been realized in recorded form, there can be no performances other than the playing of the recording, and hence no necessity for the printed page.

Electronic music has already made its way into the movies. It lends itself particularly well to situations of an eerie or otherworldly nature. An M-G-M science-fiction film, *Forbidden Planet*, employed only electronically produced sounds as its background music. But in the area of pure music, it would seem that tape recorder music will find its main province in the home. It will be heard by means of phonograph records or over the radio. There is obviously little point in a public gathering whose only purpose is to listen to a recording. In fact, the present writer can recall a certain feeling of embarrassment during the inaugural concert at the Museum of Modern Art as the audience sat there faced with nothing more than the inanimate speaker. The novelty itself may have served to diminish the strange feelings on that occasion, but it is obvious that as the novelty wears off, audiences will be less prone to listen in a public situation.

To the extent that this electronic music is accepted in homes by means of phonograph records, there will be implied something of an alteration in the attitude of the listener. Heretofore it has been understood that a phonograph recording of a conventional musical work is, of necessity, a substitute for the actual performance. The phonograph record lacks the tonal qualities that only live performers can impart. Despite the magnificent advances that have been made in recording techniques, it is only a second best. The sense of contact with the artist depends upon the listener's memories or upon his knowledge of the performer's reputation. Moreover, one of the main disadvantages of the recording of a conventional composition is its absolute predictability. Once the performance has been recorded (even though it may represent the finest version of the artist's efforts) it remains that way permanently.

None of these approaches can enter into our thinking in connection with tape recorder music. The sounds that come from the reproducing machine are not a substitute for anything; they *are* the composition, as the composer meant us to hear it. The composer writes directly for the tape and phonograph record, rather than for performance in a concert hall.

In brief, tape recorder music supplies composers with new sources of sounds, and with new ways of handling conventional sounds. To the extent that the sounds are organized, music created with the tape recorder is aesthetically as valid as is traditional music. In its elimination of the performer, it permits of a more direct communication between the composer and his audience than has been possible up to now. By the same token, though, it removes some of the very appeals that have drawn people to the more traditional music. As long as those appeals continue to exist, tape recorder music will not displace the last several hundred years of music. But it will enlarge the potential scope of music by supplying the composer with additional vocabulary.

Whether it will go down in history as merely a novel experiment or whether it will really become part of the stream of music depends ultimately upon one factor: the emergence of composers who can use the medium for the creation of emotionally convincing works.

In addition to presenting his weekly program "Music for the Connoisseur" over New York radio station WNYC and to lecturing on music appreciation to adult classes, Mr. Randolph leads his own choral group, the David Randolph Singers, and has also conducted other groups in performances of major works.

My World and What Happened to It

CONTINUED FROM PAGE 59

his way of summoning the help. You can never baffle these dukes for long. They always find a way.

Lord Emsworth, my friend continued, would no doubt do things on a somewhat more modest scale—pigging it, as it were, with a butler, an under butler, a housekeeper, a groom of the chambers, a chef, a pastry cook, some footmen, a chauffeur, a head laundrymaid, a few under laundrymaids, a head stillroom maid, some lesser stillroom maids, a squad of pantry boys, hall boys and scullery maids, and a steward's room footman.

"Golly!" I said, and my friend seemed to think well of the ejaculation. He confessed that when he allowed his mind to dwell on the human zoos he had described, he often felt like saying "Golly!" himself.

A house like that today would be staffed, I suppose, by a cook and a strong-young-girl-from-the-village to do the cleaning, and even such an entourage would probably be considered a little ostentatious. The general rule now is that the Duchess cooks and washes the dishes and the Duke dries.

So if you have no troubles of your own to worry over, you might spare the time to worry over the disappearance of the world of which I have written so much—too much, many people say—for it is not the world it was. As Kipling puts it, all our pomp of yesterday is one with Nineveh and Tyre. In a word, it has had it.

But I have not altogether lost hope of its revival. I see by the papers that the Duke of Bedford cleaned up a hundred and fifty thousand pounds last year out of those half-crowns, which is unquestionably nice sugar. If things are proceeding on similar lines all over England, the country house ought soon to be able to resume work at the old stand. Family fortunes will be restored, and Algy will get his allowance again. In other words, we may shortly have the knut with us once more.

At the moment, of course, every member of the Drones Club—and, for that matter, of Buck's, White's, and the Bachelors'—is an earnest young man immersed in some gainful pursuit who would raise his eyebrows coldly if you suggested that he pinch a policeman's helmet on Boat Race Night, but I cannot believe that this austere attitude will be permanent. The heart of Young England is sound. Give it an allowance, dangle a pair of spats before its eyes, and all the old fires will be renewed. The knut is not dead, but sleepeth.

Already one sees signs of a coming renaissance. To take but one instance, the butler is creeping back. Extinct, it seemed, only a few short years ago, he is now repeatedly seen in his old haunts like some shy bird which, driven from its native marshes by alarums and excursions, stiffens the sinews, summons up the blood, and decides to give the old home another try. True, he wants a bit more than in the golden age—ten pounds a week instead of two—but pay his price and he will buttle. In a dozen homes I know there is buttling going on just as of yore. Who can say that 'ere long spats and knuts will not be with us again?

When that happens, I shall look my critics in the eye and say, "Edwardian? Where do you get that Edwardian stuff? I write of life as it is lived today."

The Future of Machine Civilization

CONTINUED FROM PAGE 94

provide the major source of phosphorus. The waters of the seas will provide magnesium, chlorine, bromine, iodine, and sulfur. Energy will be provided by the uranium and thorium of rocks, by the rays of the sun, and conceivably by controlled thermonuclear reactions utilizing deuterium extracted from the oceans. Liquid fuels and the whole complex of organic chemicals and plastics will be produced from the carbon of limestone, utilizing either atomic energy or controlled photosynthesis—probably both.

The industries of the future will be far more complex and highly integrated than those of today. As time goes on it is likely that the single-purpose plant will diminish in importance, eventually to disappear from the scene. Increased automation will produce far-reaching effects. Unskilled and semiskilled labor will disappear. The highly trained engineer will become the "laboring man." Human control supervisors will be replaced by automatic computers. The man-hour requirements per unit of production might decrease to as little as one-tenth those of the present.

To many, these changes may seem fantastic—perhaps even impossible. But when we view the future in the perspective of both the present and the past, it seems clear that the die has been cast. We are already well along the road and it is too late to turn back. There is no way, except by the development of machine civilization, that the rapidly increasing population of the world can be supported.

World population jumped from about 500 million persons in 1650 to about 2,700 million persons in 1958. Human numbers are still increasing rapidly, but even more significant is the fact that the *rate* of increase of population is climbing rapidly as well. In the absence of a major catastrophe there does not appear to be the slightest possibility that world population will level off much below 7 billion persons. As industrialization spreads throughout the world and if our ability to produce food is indeed the population-determining factor, the number of human beings might eventually exceed even that high figure. Ten billion persons could, if necessary, be supported, but only within the framework of a culture that most of us would be reluctant to consider.

As our resources diminish in abundance and in grade, as machine civilization spreads over the world, and as human numbers continue to increase, industrial society will be confronted by a variety of problems of great complexity. Perhaps the most difficult of these problems involves the perpetuation of that society.

The vast network of mines, factories, and communication systems, upon which we have become dependent, is extremely sensitive to disruption. So interdependent are the components of the network that the sudden failure of but a relatively small section of it could result in a breakdown of the entire system. It is for this reason that machine civilization is probably far more vulnerable to disruption from nuclear attack than most persons suspect. For example, not many well-placed hydrogen bombs would be required to destroy the productive capacity of a large country such as the United States. Indeed it is quite possible that far more persons would die in the chaotic aftermath of a nuclear war as a result of the breakdown of the industrial network than would be killed directly by nuclear explosions.

Once a machine civilization has been in operation for some time, the lives of the people within the society become dependent upon the machines. The vast interlocking industrial network provides them with food, vaccines, antibiotics, and hospitals. If such a population should suddenly be deprived of a substantial fraction of its machines and forced to revert to an agrarian society, the resultant havoc would be enormous. Indeed, it is quite possible that a society within which there has been little natural selection based upon disease resistance for several generations, a society in which the people have come to depend increasingly upon surgery for repairs during early life and where there is little natural selection operating among women relative to the ability to bear children—such a society could easily become extinct in a relatively short time following the disruption of the machine network.

Indeed, a society such as that of the United States is far more vulnerable to disruption than is an agrarian society such as that of India. Most of the people of India live in small villages, each an independent economic unit producing most of the necessities of life. Cloth is woven, simple tools are manufactured, and food is produced in the surrounding countryside. Were the major cities of India to be destroyed, a large number of the villages would not be seriously affected. For this reason, should a great catastrophe strike mankind, the agrarian societies that exist at the time will clearly stand the greatest chance of inheriting the earth.

However, the underdeveloped areas of the world are themselves rapidly becoming vulnerable to disruption, for the reason that they are becoming increasingly dependent upon certain Western products for continued low mortality. Were a country such as Ceylon suddenly to find that she could no longer obtain DDT, for example, the resultant epidemic of disease would cause a burst in death rate which would almost certainly be disastrous. And as the new inexpensive techniques for control of disease spread still further, to larger countries such as India and China, the vulnerabilities of these areas to disruption will in turn grow.

It is quite possible that, so long as high-grade resources remain available in some quantity, the West itself would recover from a major war, although recovery would be a far

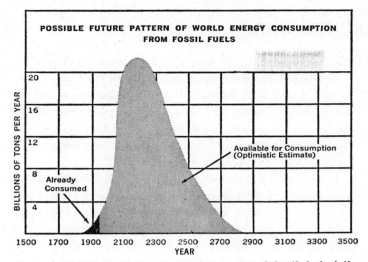

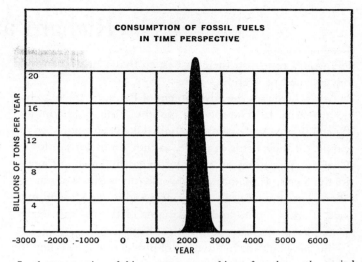

Only a small proportion of the total resources of fossil fuels (oil, coal, etc.) has yet been used up. But the fast-increasing rate of consumption may bring them close to exhaustion in about 900 years.

In the perspective of history, to say nothing of geology, the period in which man will have used up the earth's fossil fuels will look very brief—less than half the span of the Christian Era to date.

slower process than it was after World War II. But once industrial civilization has used up those high-grade resources and has become world-wide, it will be far more vulnerable.

One thing is certain: if destroyed on a world-wide basis, civilization could never be started up again by the same steps our ancestors took. Originally the spread of industrialization was facilitated by the fact that man was easily able to find vast beds of iron ore and coal, rich crystals of copper, huge deposits of petroleum, sulfur, and a variety of useful substances. But these deposits will one day be gone.

It is of course possible that, starting from a base of knowledge accumulated by a previous society and the abilities to utilize water power and to extract magnesium from sea water, man might once again learn to process rock, harness solar power, and extract energy from uranium. In such an eventuality a world-wide industrial civilization would arise once again and cover the earth. But the probabilities of a second emergence would be remote. The advantages gained by the existence of previously accumulated knowledge would probably be offset by the scarcity of the raw materials.

The situation is a little like that of a child who has been given a set of simple blocks—all the blocks of one type which exist—with which to learn to build and to make the foundation for a structure, the upper reaches of which must consist of more intricate, more difficult-to-handle forms, themselves quite unsuited for the base. If, when the foundation was built, he conserved it, he could go on building. But if he wasted and destroyed the foundation blocks, he would have "had it," as the British Royal Air Force would say. His one chance would have been squandered. His structure of the future would be a vanished dream because there would be nothing left with which to rebuild the foundation.

Our present industrialization, itself the result of a combination of no longer existent circumstances, is the only foundation on which it seems possible that a future civilization capable of utilizing the vast resources of energy now hidden in rocks and sea water and unutilized in the sun, can be built. If this foundation is destroyed, in all probability the human race has "had it."

With the consumption of each additional barrel of oil and ton of coal, with the addition of each new mouth to be fed, with the loss of each additional foot of topsoil, the situation becomes more inflexible and difficult to resolve. If we continue to think only of the present and ignore the future, it is quite likely that we shall paint ourselves into a corner from which it will be impossible to extricate ourselves.

Yet the unpleasant outcomes that are indicated by the existing trends are by no means inevitable. If we make full use of the powers of conceptual thought with which we are endowed, we should be able to avoid catastrophe. We have seen that in spite of the fact that our high-grade resources are disappearing, given adequate energy resources we can live comfortably on low-grade resources. Further, it seems clear that man has available potential sources of energy which are sufficient to satisfy his needs for a very long time in the future. We have also seen that, although a large fraction of the world's population is starving, there appear to be no technological barriers to the feeding of a stable world population several times the present size. We know that, although world populations are increasing rapidly, population growth can in principle be stopped. Indeed, it is amply clear that man can, if he wills it, create a world in which human beings can live comfortably and in peace with each other.

If we fail this challenge there is every likelihood that our civilization will perish—never to reappear.

Harrison Brown is professor of geochemistry at the California Institute of Technology. Here he develops some of his ideas presented in The Challenge of Man's Future, *published by Viking Press, Inc.*

Richard and Saladin

CONTINUED FROM PAGE 91

lers would return to their castles, so that Christians would have armed protection.

As a scheme for the government of Palestine the plan had great merits. In the proposed realm of King Saphadin and Queen Joan, Arab peasants, both Christian and Moslem, would till their fields in peace, as they do in Jordan today; Christian pilgrims would visit Jerusalem and go home again; in the ports, Italian traders would do business under an alien government, as in Alexandria and other Moslem markets. Turkish emirs and the knights of the military orders would keep the peace in open country.

But the plan was in advance of public opinion. When the Crusaders heard of it they were deeply shocked, so shocked that the loyal English compiler of the *Itinerarium Regis Ricardi* does not mention it. Joan, furious, announced that she would never marry a Moslem. Then Richard asked Saphadin whether he would consider turning Christian and got the answer he must have expected. Saladin chuckled to see the champion of the Cross in such a false position. He at once made things more difficult by giving his solemn assent, and then sat back to see how Richard would extricate himself.

To save his darling project, Richard offered his niece Eleanor of Brittany in place of Joan, but Saphadin would accept no substitute. The scheme was buried. Richard advanced to Beit-Nuba, within twelve miles of Jerusalem, but changed his mind and marched south to Ascalon. That gave him a valuable bargaining counter; a Christian army at Ascalon could cut the road between Syria and Egypt, severing Saladin's recruiting ground from his principal source of revenue.

Therefore, at the end of March, Saladin for the first time made overtures for peace, instead of waiting for Richard's envoys. Saphadin came down to Ascalon with an offer: the Franks might have all the coast cities they had conquered and in addition the harbor of Beirut; they would enjoy free access to the Holy Sepulchre, and as a bonus, the True Cross would be returned. For a fortnight Saphadin was entertained as Richard's guest, and during the festivities Richard knighted his son. But the negotiations petered out.

Reports had reached Richard of his brother's constant encroachment in England. But before he could leave the Holy Land, he had to settle the rivalry between King Guy and Conrad. King Guy consented to abdicate, taking Cyprus as compensation; then Conrad, the unanimous choice of the barons, was murdered by Assassins (the followers of the Old Man of the Mountain whose motive for the crime is still obscure). Eventually a compromise candidate was found, nephew to both King Richard and King Philip. When Henry of Champagne was proclaimed king of Jerusalem, Richard at last had the support of every Frank in Outremer. To cement his claim Henry married Isabella,

then twenty-one, seven days after her husband's death.

In June, Richard led his united army for the second time to Beit-Nuba, only to learn that the wells between Beit-Nuba and Jerusalem had been destroyed. His army could not live without water, so in July he retired to Jaffa. From thence he sent envoys to Saladin; at last the long negotiation seemed to be leading to a settlement.

If Richard would evacuate Ascalon, Saladin offered not only peace but friendship with the new King Henry: the Franks might dwell undisturbed on the coast and their priests could minister in the Holy Places. Richard still argued, hoping to gain these terms and keep Ascalon too, but peace seemed so near that he moved north two weeks later to Acre, planning to embark for Europe.

Suddenly Saladin swooped on weakly held Jaffa, marching down from Jerusalem in one day, July 27. Since Arsuf, in the previous September, he had been on the defensive, and Richard was taken unawares. Within three days the Moslems breached the town wall, and the small garrison retreated to the castle. But Richard hastened to the rescue.

In the chapter of accidents that followed, Saladin was an eyewitness to the deeds of the Christian hero, though still the two leaders never met in a parley. Richard left Acre by sea, while his army marched south by the coast road. When he was delayed by contrary winds his army, not wishing to fight without him, loitered on the march. On the thirty-first he reached Jaffa, only to see Moslem banners on the town wall. He thought he had come too late, but a brave priest swam out from the beleaguered castle and explained the situation. Richard had with him only eighty dismounted knights, a handful of crossbows, and the Italian sailors of his ships. He waded ashore, and with this small force drove the Moslems from Jaffa.

Next morning Saladin sent his chamberlain to seek peace, still offering large concessions in return for Ascalon. Abu Bekr found Richard joking with some captured emirs, explaining that Jaffa had been guaranteed to hold out for three months—yet Saladin had taken it in three days and he, Richard, had won it back in three hours. He had hurried so fast to the fight that he had charged still wearing his boating slippers.

Richard would not yield Ascalon, but he offered to hold it as a fief under Saladin. This might have worked if there had been a genuine peace: there was no compelling reason why Christian knights should not fight for Saladin against his Moslem enemies. But Saladin did not trust feudal tenures, and the offer was refused.

Richard and his escort encamped outside the walls of Jaffa, for the town was littered with unburied dead. The Moslems, while killing the unarmed citizens, had also killed all the pigs, and fragments of pork had been deliberately

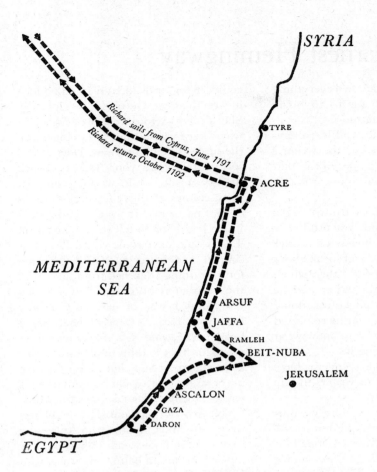

SYRIA

TYRE

ACRE

Richard sails from Cyprus, June 1191

Richard returns October 1192

MEDITERRANEAN
SEA

ARSUF

JAFFA

RAMLEH

BEIT-NUBA

JERUSALEM

ASCALON

GAZA

DARON

EGYPT

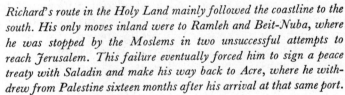

Richard's route in the Holy Land mainly followed the coastline to the south. His only moves inland were to Ramleh and Beit-Nuba, where he was stopped by the Moslems in two unsuccessful attempts to reach Jerusalem. This failure eventually forced him to sign a peace treaty with Saladin and make his way back to Acre, where he withdrew from Palestine sixteen months after his arrival at that same port.

mingled with fragments of Christians; so burial was a slow process. The Frankish army had still not arrived when, on August 5, Saladin made a sudden assault on the unwalled bivouac.

Richard had about 2,000 men, and only fifteen horses. With this force he withstood the attack of 7,000 Turkish cavalry. In the afternoon Saladin, watching from his usual post with the reserve, saw Richard counterattack. Then suddenly the King of England was down, his horse killed under him. Overwhelmed by such a display of courage, Saladin made the noblest gesture of his life. Through the thick of battle he sent a groom, leading two horses as a gift to his brave enemy. At the end of the day the Moslems marched back in good order to Jerusalem.

Negotiations began again. The usual presents were exchanged: fruit and snow for Western hawks and hounds. In the end Richard agreed to evacuate Ascalon, after dismantling its fortifications. In return Saladin promised five years of peace. Pilgrims would be welcome in Jerusalem and Latin priests might serve in the Holy Places, Nazareth and Bethlehem as well as the Sepulchre. Most important of all,

because Outremer needed the ships and trade of Italian merchants, Moslems would be free to trade with the Christian ports.

The treaty was signed on September 2. At once a crowd of Western Crusaders visited the Sepulchre and then took the next ship home; Moslem emirs visited Jaffa to spend their pay on Western trinkets, and then returned to Saladin. That had been from the beginning Richard's handicap; his men would go home when they had fulfilled the pilgrimage, but Saladin's men were already at home.

Richard refused the humiliation of an unarmed visit to Jerusalem; on October 9 he embarked. Before leaving he sent a last message to Saladin, boasting that when the five years of peace were over he would come back to storm the Holy City. Saladin answered courteously that he would do his best to hold it, but that if God willed otherwise, Richard was the man most worthy to conquer it.

Saladin had retained his conquests at the cost of his life. He died on March 4, 1193, in his fifty-fifth year, worn out by his exertions. His heirs were his seventeen sons; but by 1201, Saphadin, that experienced, cosmopolitan diplomatist, had displaced them all and ruled over Syria and Egypt.

As king of England Richard was a failure; only in Outremer did he show himself a statesman. His plan for a neutral kingdom of Jerusalem might have satisfied all parties if he could have persuaded his sister to marry a Moslem. He perceived that military victory was within his reach and that military victory would dissolve his army. Then he perceived that Ascalon would be a standing threat to Saladin. To the end he bargained boldly and saved what could be saved—a thin strip ninety miles long and less than ten miles wide. But because he had given it an indispensable base in Cyprus, the kingdom of Jerusalem endured for another century. Of how many statesmen can it be said that their gains endure for a hundred years? And besides his achievements as a diplomatist and general, Richard was personally the best warrior in his army.

Saladin was no warrior. But he could recognize gallantry in others, and his gesture to Richard outside Jaffa is something in which both Christian and Moslem may take pride. In all these lengthy negotiations neither was ever accused of double-dealing; neither broke his pledged word. What is more, neither tried to convert the other. Islam and Christendom must always be foes, but wise men may fix up a local truce on a disputed boundary. As we watch the gyrations of those who wish to settle the whole Cold War at one conference, we should remember that long ago two brave soldiers brought peace to a patch of land. Because they agreed to differ on essentials, they managed to work out a limited local compromise.

One of England's leading historical novelists, Alfred Duggan has written of Richard's medieval England in Devil's Brood *and* My Life for My Sheep, *and of the First Crusade in* Knight With Armor.

An Interview with Ernest Hemingway

CONTINUED FROM PAGE 85

INTERVIEWER: Would you suggest newspaper work for the young writer? How helpful was the training you had with the *Kansas City Star?*

HEMINGWAY: On the *Star* you were forced to learn to write a simple declarative sentence. This is useful to anyone. Newspaper work will not harm a young writer and could help him if he gets out of it in time. This is one of the dustiest clichés there is and I apologize for it. But when you ask someone old, tired questions you are apt to receive old, tired answers.

INTERVIEWER: You once wrote in the *Transatlantic Review* that the only reason for writing journalism was to be well paid. You said: "And when you destroy the valuable things you have by writing about them, you want to get big money for it." Do you think of writing as a type of self-destruction?

HEMINGWAY: I do not remember ever writing that. But it sounds silly and violent enough for me to have said it to avoid having to bite on the nail and make a sensible statement. I certainly do not think of writing as a type of self-destruction, though journalism, after a point has been reached, can be a daily self-destruction for a serious creative writer.

INTERVIEWER: Do you think the intellectual stimulus of the company of other writers is of any value to an author?

HEMINGWAY: Certainly.

INTERVIEWER: In the Paris of the twenties did you have any sense of "group feeling" with other writers and artists?

HEMINGWAY: No. There was no group feeling. We had respect for each other. I respected a lot of painters, some of my own age, others older: Gris, Picasso, Braque, Monet, who was still alive then, and a few writers: Joyce, Ezra, the good of Stein . . .

INTERVIEWER: When you are writing do you ever find yourself influenced by what you're reading at the time?

HEMINGWAY: Not since Joyce was writing *Ulysses*. His was not a direct influence. But in those days when words we knew were barred to us and we had to fight for a single word, the influence of his work was what changed everything and made it possible for us to break away from the restrictions.

INTERVIEWER: Could you learn anything about writing from the writers? You were telling me yesterday that Joyce, for example, couldn't bear to talk about writing.

HEMINGWAY: In company with people of your own trade you ordinarily speak of other writers' books. The better the writers the less they will speak about what they have written themselves. Joyce was a very great writer and he would only explain what he was doing to jerks. Other writers that he respected were supposed to be able to know what he was doing by reading it.

INTERVIEWER: You seem to have avoided the company of writers in late years. Why?

HEMINGWAY: That is more complicated. The further you go in writing the more alone you are. Most of your best and oldest friends die. Others move away. You do not see them except rarely, but you write and have much the same contact with them as though you were together at the café in the old days. You exchange comic, sometimes cheerfully obscene, and irresponsible letters, and it is almost as good as talking. But you are more alone because that is how you must work and the time to work is shorter all the time and if you waste it you feel you have committed a sin for which there is no forgiveness.

INTERVIEWER: What about the influence of some of these people—your contemporaries—on your work? What was Gertrude Stein's contribution, if any? or Ezra Pound's? or Max Perkins'?

HEMINGWAY: I'm sorry but I am no good at these post-mortems. There are coroners literary and nonliterary provided to deal with such matters. Miss Stein wrote at some length and with considerable inaccuracy about her influence on my work. It was necessary for her to do this after she had learned to write dialogue from a book called *The Sun Also Rises*. I was very fond of her and thought it was splendid she had learned to write conversation. It was no new thing to me to learn from everyone I could, living or dead, and I had no idea it would affect Gertrude so violently. She already wrote very well in other ways. Ezra was extremely intelligent on the subjects he really knew. Doesn't this sort of talk bore you? This backyard literary gossip while washing out the dirty clothes of thirty-five years ago is disgusting to me. It would be different if one had tried to tell the whole truth. That would have some value. Here it is simpler and better to thank Gertrude for everything I learned from her about the abstract relationship of words, say how fond I was of her, reaffirm my loyalty to Ezra as a great poet and a loyal friend, and say that I cared so much for Max Perkins that I have never been able to accept that he is dead. He never asked me to change anything I wrote except to remove certain words which were not then publishable. Blanks were left, and anyone who knew the words would know what they were. For me he was not an editor. He was a wise friend and a wonderful companion. I liked the way he wore his hat and the strange way his lips moved.

INTERVIEWER: Who would you say are your literary forebears—those you have learned the most from?

HEMINGWAY: Mark Twain, Flaubert, Stendhal, Bach, Turgenev, Tolstoi, Dostoyevsky, Chekhov, Andrew Marvell, John Donne, Maupassant, the good Kipling, Thoreau, Captain Marryat, Shakespeare, Mozart, Quevedo, Dante, Virgil, Tintoretto, Hieronymus Bosch, Breugel, Patinir, Goya, Giotto, Cézanne, Van Gogh, Gauguin, San Juan de la Cruz, Góngora—it would take a day to remember everyone. Then it would sound as though I were claiming an erudition I did not possess instead of trying to remember all the people who have been an influence on my life and work. This isn't an old, dull question. It is a very good but a solemn question and requires an examination of conscience. I put in painters, or started to, because I learn as much from painters about how to write as from writers. You ask how this is done? It would take another day of explaining. I should think what one learns from composers and from the study of harmony and counterpoint would be obvious.

INTERVIEWER: Did you ever play a musical instrument?

HEMINGWAY: I used to play cello. My mother kept me out of school a whole year to study music and counterpoint. She thought I had ability, but I was absolutely without talent. We played chamber music—someone came in to play the violin, my sister played the viola, and mother the piano. That cello —I played it worse than anyone on earth. Of course, that year I was out doing other things too.

INTERVIEWER: Do you reread the authors of your list? Twain, for instance?

HEMINGWAY: You have to wait two or three years with Twain. You remember too well. I read some Shakespeare every year, *Lear* always. Cheers you up if you read that.

INTERVIEWER: Well, could we go back to that list and take one of the painters—Hieronymus Bosch, for instance? The nightmare symbolic quality of his work seems so far removed from your own.

HEMINGWAY: I have the nightmares and know about the ones other people have. But you do not have to write them down. Anything you can omit that you know you still have in the writing and its quality will show. When a writer omits things he does not know, they show like holes in his writing.

INTERVIEWER: Does that mean that a close knowledge of the works of the people on your list helps fill the "well" you were speaking of a while back? Or were they consciously a help in developing the techniques of writing?

HEMINGWAY: They were a part of learning to see, to hear, to think, to feel and not feel, and to write. The well is where your juice is. Nobody knows what it is made of, least of all yourself. What you know is if you have it, or you have to wait for it to come back.

INTERVIEWER: Would you admit to there being symbolism in your novels?

HEMINGWAY: I suppose there are symbols since critics keep finding them. If you do not mind, I dislike talking about them and being questioned about them. It is hard enough to write books and stories without being asked to explain them as well. Also it deprives the explainers of work. If five or six or more good explainers can keep going why should I interfere with them? Read anything I write for the pleasure of reading it. Whatever else you find will be the measure of what you brought to the reading.

INTERVIEWER: I remember you have warned that it is dangerous for a writer to talk about a work in progress, that he can "talk it out" so to speak. Why should this be so? I only ask because there are so many writers—Twain, Wilde, Thurber, Steffens come to mind —who would seem to have polished their material by testing it on listeners.

HEMINGWAY: I cannot believe Twain ever "tested out" *Huckleberry Finn* on listeners. If he did they probably had him cut out good things and put in the bad parts. Wilde was said by people who knew him to have been a better talker than a writer. Steffens talked better than he wrote. Both his writing and his talking were sometimes hard to believe, and I heard many stories change as he grew older. If Thurber can talk as well as he writes he must be one of the greatest and least boring talkers. The man I know who talks best about his own trade and has the pleasantest and most wicked tongue is Juan Belmonte, the matador.

INTERVIEWER: Could you say how much thought-out effort went into the evolvement of your distinctive style?

HEMINGWAY: That is a long-term, tiring question and if you spent a couple of days answering it you would be so self-conscious that you could not write. I might say that what amateurs call a style is usually only the unavoidable awkwardnesses in first trying to make something that has not heretofore been made. People think these awkwardnesses are the style and many copy them. This is regrettable.

INTERVIEWER: You once wrote me that the simple circumstances under which various pieces of fiction were written could be instructive. Could you apply this to *The Killers*—you said that you had written it, *Ten Indians*, and *Today is Friday* in one day—and perhaps to your first novel *The Sun Also Rises?*

HEMINGWAY: Let's see. *The Sun Also Rises* I started in Valencia on my birthday, July 21. Hadley, my wife, and I had gone to Valencia early to get good tickets for the *Feria* there which started the twenty-fourth of July. Everybody my age had written a novel and I was still having a difficult time writing a paragraph. So I started the book on my birthday, wrote all through the *Feria*, in bed in the morning, went on to Madrid and wrote there. There was no *Feria* there, so we had a room with a table and I wrote in great luxury on the table and around the corner from the hotel in a beer place in the Pasaje Alvarez where it was cool. It finally got too hot to write and we went to Hendaye. There was a small cheap hotel there on the big long lovely beach and I worked very well there and then went up to Paris and finished the first draft in the apartment over the sawmill at 113 rue Notre-Dame-des-Champs six weeks from the day I started it. I showed the first draft to Nathan Asch, the novelist, who then had quite a strong accent and he said, "Hem, vaht do you mean saying you wrote a novel? A novel huh. Hem you are riding a travhel büch." I was not too discouraged by Nathan and rewrote the book, keeping in the travel (that was the part about the fishing trip and Pamplona) at Schruns in the Vorarlberg at the Hotel Taube.

The stories you mention I wrote in one day in Madrid on May 16 when it snowed out the San Isidro bullfights. First I wrote *The Killers*, which I'd tried to write before and failed. Then after lunch I got in bed to keep warm and wrote *Today is Friday*. I had so much juice I thought maybe I was going crazy and I had about six other stories to write. So I got dressed and walked to Fornos, the old bullfighter's café, and drank coffee and then came back and wrote *Ten Indians*. This made me very sad and I drank some brandy and went to sleep. I'd forgotten to eat and one of the waiters brought me up some *bacalao* and a small steak and fried potatoes and a bottle of Valdepeñas.

The woman who ran the *pension* was always worried that I did not eat enough and she had sent the waiter. I remember sitting up in bed and eating, and drinking the Valdepeñas. The waiter said he would bring up another bottle. He said the Señora wanted to know if I was going to write all night. I said no, I thought I would lay off for a while. Why don't you try to write just one more, the waiter asked. I'm only supposed to write one, I said. Nonsense, he said. You could write six. I'll try tomorrow, I said. Try it tonight, he said. What do you think the old woman sent the food up for?

I'm tired, I told him. Nonsense, he said (the word was not nonsense). You tired after three miserable little stories. Translate me one.

Leave me alone, I said. How am I going to write it if you don't leave me alone. So I sat up in bed and drank the Valdepeñas and thought what a hell of a writer I was if the first story was as good as I'd hoped.

INTERVIEWER: How complete in your own mind is the conception of a short story? Does the theme, or the plot, or a character change as you go along?

HEMINGWAY: Sometimes you know the story. Sometimes you make it up as you go along and have no idea how it will come out. Everything changes as it moves. That is what makes the movement which makes the story. Sometimes the movement is so slow it does not seem to be moving. But there is always change and always movement.

INTERVIEWER: Is it the same with the novel, or do you work out the whole plan before you start and adhere to it rigorously?

HEMINGWAY: *For Whom the Bell Tolls* was a problem which I carried on each day. I knew what was going to happen in principle. But I invented what happened each day I wrote.

INTERVIEWER: Do you find it easy to shift from one literary project to another or do you continue through to finish what you start?

HEMINGWAY: The fact that I am interrupting serious work to answer these questions proves that I am so stupid that I should be penalized severely. I will be. Don't worry.

INTERVIEWER: We've not discussed character. Are the characters of your work taken without exception from real life?

HEMINGWAY: Of course they are not. *Some* come from real life. Mostly you invent people from a knowledge and understanding and experience of people.

INTERVIEWER: Could you say something about the process of turning a real-life character into a fictional one?

HEMINGWAY: If I explained how that is sometimes done, it would be a handbook for libel lawyers.

INTERVIEWER: Do you make a distinction—as E. M. Forster does—between "flat" and "round" characters?

HEMINGWAY: If you describe someone, it is flat, as a photograph is, and from my standpoint a failure. If you make him up from what you know, there should be all the dimensions.

INTERVIEWER: Do the titles come to you while you're in the process of doing the story?

HEMINGWAY: No. I make a list of titles *after* I've finished the story or the book—sometimes as many as one hundred. Then I start eliminating them, sometimes all of them.

INTERVIEWER: And you do this even with a story whose title is supplied from the text—*Hills Like White Elephants*, for example?

HEMINGWAY: Yes. The title comes afterwards. I met a girl in Prunier where I'd gone to eat oysters before lunch. I knew she'd had an abortion. I went over and we talked, not about that, but on the way home I thought of the story, skipped lunch, and spent that afternoon writing it.

INTERVIEWER: So when you're not writing, you remain constantly the observer, looking for something which can be of use.

HEMINGWAY: Surely. If a writer stops observing he is finished. But he does not have to observe consciously nor think how it will be useful. Perhaps that would be true at the beginning. But later everything he sees goes into the great reserve of things he knows or has seen. If it is any use to know it, I always try to write on the principle of the iceberg. There is seven-eighths of it underwater for every part that shows. Anything you know you can eliminate and it only strengthens your iceberg. It is the part that doesn't show. If a writer omits something because he does not know it then there is a hole in the story.

The Old Man and the Sea could have been over a thousand pages long and had every character in the village in it and all the processes of how they made their living, were born, educated, bore children, etc. That is done excellently and well by other writers. In writing you are limited by what has already

been done satisfactorily. So I have tried to learn to do something else. First I have tried to eliminate everything unnecessary to conveying experience to the reader so that after he or she has read something it will become a part of his or her experience and seem actually to have happened. This is very hard to do and I've worked at it very hard.

Anyway, to skip how it is done, I had unbelievable luck this time and could convey the experience completely and have it be one that no one had ever conveyed. The luck was that I had a good man and a good boy and lately writers have forgotten there still are such things. Then the ocean is worth writing about just as man is. So I was lucky there. I've seen the marlin mate and know about that. So I leave that out. I've seen a school (or pod) of more than fifty sperm whales in that same stretch of water and once harpooned one nearly sixty feet in length and lost him. So I left that out. All the stories I know from the fishing village I leave out. But the knowledge is what makes the underwater part of the iceberg.

INTERVIEWER: Archibald MacLeish has spoken of a method of conveying experience to a reader which he said you developed while covering baseball games back in those *Kansas City Star* days. It was simply that experience is communicated by small details, intimately preserved, which have the effect of indicating the whole by making the reader conscious of what he had been aware of only subconsciously . . .

HEMINGWAY: The anecdote is apocryphal. I never wrote baseball for the *Star*. What Archie was trying to remember was how I was trying to learn in Chicago around 1920 and was searching for the unnoticed things that made emotions such as the way an outfielder tossed his glove without looking back to where it fell, the squeak of resin on canvas under a fighter's flat-soled gym shoes, the gray color of Jack Blackburn's skin when he had just come out of stir, and other things I noted as a painter sketches. You saw Blackburn's strange color and the old razor cuts and the way he spun a man before you knew his history. These were the things which moved you before you knew the story.

INTERVIEWER: Have you ever described any type of situation of which you had no personal knowledge?

HEMINGWAY: That is a strange question. By personal knowledge do you mean carnal knowledge? In that case the answer is positive. A writer, if he is any good, does not describe. He invents or *makes* out of knowledge personal and impersonal, and sometimes he seems to have unexplained knowledge which could come from forgotten racial or family experience. Who teaches the homing pigeon to fly as he does; where does a fighting bull get his bravery or a hunting dog his nose? This is an elaboration or a condensation on that stuff we were talking in Madrid that time when my head was not to be trusted.

INTERVIEWER: How detached must you be from an experience before you can write about it in fictional terms? The African air crashes, for instance?

HEMINGWAY: It depends on the experience. One part of you sees it with complete detachment from the start. Another part is very involved. I think there is no rule about how soon one should write about it. It would depend on how well adjusted the individual was and on his or her recuperative powers. Certainly it is valuable to a trained writer to crash in an aircraft which burns. He learns several important things very quickly. Whether they will be of use to him is conditioned by survival. Survival, with honor, that outmoded and all-important word, is as difficult as ever and as all-important to a writer. Those who do not last are always more beloved since no one has to see them in their long, dull, unrelenting, no-quarter-given and no-quarter-received fights that they make to do something as they believe it should be done before they die. Those who die or quit early and easy and with every good reason are preferred because they are understandable and human.

Failure and well-disguised cowardice are more human and more beloved.

INTERVIEWER: Could I ask you to what extent you think the writer should concern himself with the socio-political problems of his times?

HEMINGWAY: Everyone has his own conscience and there should be no rules about how a conscience should function. All you can be sure about in a political-minded writer is that if his work should last you will have to skip the politics when you read it. Many of the so-called politically enlisted writers change their politics frequently. This is very exciting to them and to their political-literary reviews. Sometimes they even have to re-write their viewpoints—and in a hurry. Perhaps it can be respected as a form of the pursuit of happiness.

INTERVIEWER: Did the political influence of Ezra Pound on the segregationalist Kasper have any effect on your belief that the poet ought to be released from St. Elizabeth's Hospital?

HEMINGWAY: No. None at all. I believed Ezra should be released and allowed to write poetry in Italy on an undertaking by him to abstain from any politics. Great poets are not necessarily girl guides nor scoutmasters nor splendid influences on youth. To name a few: Verlaine, Rimbaud, Shelley, Byron, Baudelaire, Proust, Gide should not have been confined to prevent them from being aped in their thinking, their manners, or their morals by local Kaspers. I am sure that it will take a footnote to this paragraph in ten years to explain who Kasper was.*

INTERVIEWER: It has been said that a writer only deals with one or two ideas throughout his work. Would you say

*John Kasper was convicted of contempt of court in 1957 for efforts to prevent integration at the Clinton, Tennessee, high school and sentenced to a prison term.

your work reflects one or two ideas?

HEMINGWAY: Who said that? It sounds much too simple. The man who said it possibly *had* only one or two ideas.

INTERVIEWER: Well, perhaps it would be better put this way: Graham Greene has said that a ruling passion gives to a shelf of novels the unity of a system. You yourself have said, I believe, that great writing comes out of a sense of injustice. Do you consider it important that a novelist be dominated in this way —by some such compelling sense?

HEMINGWAY: Mr. Greene has a facility for making statements that I do not possess. It would be impossible for me to make generalizations about a shelf of novels or a wisp of snipe or a gaggle of geese. I'll try a generalization though. A writer without a sense of justice and of injustice would be better off editing the yearbook of a school for exceptional children than writing novels. Another generalization. You see; they are not so difficult when they are sufficiently obvious. The most essential gift for a good writer is a built-in, shock-proof crap detector. This is the writer's radar and all great writers have had it.

INTERVIEWER: Finally, a fundamental question: namely, as a creative writer what do you think is the function of your art? Why a representation of fact, rather than fact itself?

HEMINGWAY: Why be puzzled by that? From things that have happened and from things as they exist and from all things that you know and all those you cannot know, you make something through your invention that is not a representation but a whole new thing truer than anything true and alive, and you make it alive, and if you make it well enough, you give it immortality. That is why you write and for no other reason that you know of. But what about all the reasons that no one knows?

The Great Engineer: Isambard Kingdom Brunel

CONTINUED FROM PAGE 42

For the greater part of her long life, the *Great Britain* was on the run to Australia, but as she had been designed for the Atlantic service, this much longer voyage involved bunkering at the Cape with steam coal specially sent out for her by sailing ship from South Wales. It was with the object of avoiding such costly refueling that Brunel designed the third and last of his great ships, the fabulous *Great Eastern*.

With a displacement of 32,000 tons—four times the size of any ship afloat at that time—Brunel's great ship could steam around the world without refueling. In her huge iron hull, double-skinned and immensely strong, her designer incorporated all the experience he had gained from his two earlier ships. It was his final engineering masterpiece and stands out as a landmark in the history of shipbuilding. Alas! In designing a ship which was not to be surpassed in size until 1899, Brunel jumped too far ahead of his time. Although two sets of engines were installed—one driving a screw and the other, huge paddle wheels—in those days of low-pressure steam it was impossible to provide enough power to drive so large a hull. Though her engines were the largest ever built and indicated 10,000 horsepower, the *Great Eastern* disappointed in speed.

Because the building site made an end-on launch out of the question, the *Great Eastern* had been laid down parallel with the riverbank. This meant that a hull weighing over 12,000 tons had to be pushed sideways down special launching ways until it could be floated off on a spring tide. Cruel circumstances compelled Brunel to undertake this gigantic task with inadequate equipment at the worst season of the year. Hydraulic rams burst and heavy chain cables parted like threads, but ultimately, after three months' struggle, the ship was successfully floated on the last day of January, 1858. But this success had been purchased at a terrible price: Brunel's health was ruined, and the company could not finance the fitting out of his ship.

In the spring of 1859 a new company was formed to complete the *Great Eastern*, and Brunel, though mortally ill and prematurely aged, personally superintended the work of getting his monster ready for sea. A cabin had been reserved for him for the maiden voyage that would set the seal on all his efforts, but he never achieved this last ambition. Two days before his ship was due to sail he collapsed on her deck. He had suffered a stroke that left him partially paralyzed. So, on September 7, the *Great Eastern* left without him. She was off Dungeness on her course down channel when disaster struck. Owing to inexcusable carelessness on the part of the builder, John Scott Russell, and his men who were in charge of the paddle engines and their boilers, a feed-water heater exploded. It blew one of the huge funnels into the air, wrecked the grand saloon, and scalded to death six firemen. The ship was able to proceed to Weymouth as planned, but the effect of the disaster on Brunel, who lay waiting for news at his home, was tragic. Even his indomitable spirit was broken by the news of this crowning misfortune, and a few days later, on September 15, 1859, Brunel died.

As a passenger ship the *Great Eastern* was never a success. Owing to changes in world trade and the opening of the Suez Canal, through which, as first built, she was too large to pass, Brunel's great ship could never be used on the Australia run for which she was designed. Instead she ran to New York but was too big for the North Atlantic trade of that time. It was Daniel Gooch who vindicated both the ship and her designer by equipping her for cable laying, in which capacity she was outstandingly successful. With Gooch himself on board, the *Great Eastern* laid the first transatlantic cable from Valencia to Newfoundland, and she then went on to weave a web of cables around the world.

So ended the career of an extraordinary personality, a career of commercial failure but of engineering triumph. The man and his three great ships are now only a memory, but today, on the eve of the centenary of his death, his railway works still stand for later generations to marvel at. Moreover, no man contributed more than did Brunel to the task of forging those links of transport and communication that tie the two halves of the English-speaking world together.

Aside from his material achievement, what we should most admire about Brunel in our overspecialized age is the astonishing versatility of intellect and imagination that ranged so freely and with such assurance over the whole field of art and science. He reminds us that there was then no gulf fixed between the arts and sciences, and he makes us reflect a little sadly that the world might be a better place today if that gulf had never opened and man had not grown so specialized an animal, knowing more and more about less and less.

The best of all memorials to Isambard Kingdom Brunel are the words written in a diary by that friend who had always shown him such unswerving loyalty and who now mourned his loss. "On the 15th September," wrote Daniel Gooch, "I lost my oldest and best friend. . . . By his death the greatest of England's engineers was lost, the man with the greatest originality of thought and power of execution, bold in his plans but right. The commercial world thought him extravagant; but although he was so, great things are not done by those who sit and count the cost of every thought and act."

L.T.C. Rolt is a former mechanical engineer turned author who has averaged a book a year since 1944. Isambard Kingdom Brunel *and* Thomas Telford, *biographies of rival engineers, are his latest.*

THE TYRANNY OF THE TEENS

America's well-heeled adolescents are the best customers for movies, radio, and records—and the cus-

tomers get what they want. But what will be left of popular culture by the time they're twenty?

By WILLIAM K. ZINSSER

One night last summer, in one of those sleepy Long Island towns that only the hurricanes can find, my wife and I were sitting on the glider—we bought an old house and converted it into a barn—when a wild impulse seized us. We decided to go to the movies and see Elvis Presley in *King Creole*. The picture had been in town all week, and the stamp of its star was heavy on Main Street. From huge posters the puffy young balladeer gazed out at the passing citizens, as he presumably gazed out at a thousand other main streets across America that evening, exerting the strange spell that has made him, in only a few hideous years, one of our nation's reigning millionaires.

Somehow the face did not excite my blood beyond its usual 98.6 as I strolled past it, day after day, on my way to the general store, nor did the fact that Presley in motion is regarded as one of nature's most intoxicating displays. If anything, the face made me wish that some day the theater would get around to showing a movie that adults could also enjoy. *High School Confidential* had been there the previous week, and it in turn had followed various other exer-

cises in horror and assault as practiced by the younger set, such as *I Was a Teen-Age Frankenstein*.

But that night on the porch some nameless urge made us want to see a movie. Perhaps it was because the glider was broken and had done little gliding since its Victorian youth. Perhaps it was the vestigial movie-going instinct, which survives even when we cross out of our teens into the twenties and thirties, though Hollywood seems to lose interest in us then. In any case, I bolted a few ounces of bourbon, hoping to match in my own fashion the giddy state which the rest of the audience would achieve simply by looking at Presley, and soon we were settled in our seats at the Playhouse.

A newsreel was in progress, with its usual diet of war and disaster, so I peered around in the dark to see my adolescent neighbors. To my surprise, the theater was almost empty. Here and there I spotted a middle-aged couple, a white-haired lady, and such staid local merchants as the butcher, the baker, and the candlestick-maker. (The town happens to have a big trade in candlesticks.) But of America's youth there was none. Among the dim heads I saw no female ponytail, no male pompadour, no profile that looked even partly juvenile, or even delinquent. A wave of relief surged through me. Obviously the Presley bubble had burst at last, and his worshipers had gone to follow another piper. The older people in the theater were probably there by mistake, thinking *King Creole* a quaint travelogue of New Orleans.

The newsreel ended with the customary fire in the oil refinery, and *King Creole* came on, looking very much like a quaint travelogue of New Orleans. Shrimp vendors sang old street cries to housewives in the windows above. Suddenly, in one of these windows, there appeared a sullen young man with heavy eyes, whom I recognized instantly as Elvis Presley. He was undulating slightly, as if some invisible reducing belt were gently massaging his hips, and this may have helped me to identify him so quickly.

But the biggest help, I suppose, was the fact that there rose from the balcony of the movie house—I didn't even know it *had* a balcony—the ecstatic squeals of countless young things in ripest girlhood. I hazarded a guess that an equal number of boys were attending these tribal rites upstairs. From this I could only conclude that the Presley bubble had not burst after all. The faithful were densely packed in the balcony, leaving the rest of the theater to us infidels—the old and the square.

King Creole turned out to be a shrewd blend of two elements that teen-agers hold dear—violence and rock-'n'-roll. It had enough muggings and rumbles to gratify any apprentice hoodlum, and these kept the story moving when Presley was not crooning one of his feverish odes. He sang about fifteen altogether, though it didn't seem like more than twenty, in a variety of musical and clothing styles, all of them lush beyond normal standards of voice and dress.

At some point in each song the balcony girls broke into their adoring shrieks. The point varied in each number, and I could never see what signal touched the young ladies off. Presley might, for example, rotate his body in the manner that has brought the moniker "Elvis the Pelvis" into the living language of our land, and I would think: "Aha! That'll drive 'em flippo." I would squeal, just to prove I was from Hepville, and squeal alone. Silence drenched the balcony. Then, at some point when Presley's delivery seemed ordinary, if not downright dull, Young America started keening upstairs. The same thing happened in each of Presley's songs. Even my wife, who is in her mid-twenties and thus not far beyond the boundaries of Teenland as a life span is counted, could not judge the moment of truth. It was transmitted by a secret code—a code that is erased from the ken of mortals when they come to the end of their nineteenth year.

The evening did not really surprise me. I expected as much. I am resigned to the fact that teen-agers dictate most of the popular tastes in America today, that we adults are mere visitors tiptoeing about in their world. When teen-agers speak up, the merchants listen, and if there's one thing that teen-agers do nowadays, it's speak up. No week goes by without an article in a major magazine called "Teen-agers Speak Up!" Youth never tires of telling us why they go steady, dress funny, love Elvis, hate their parents, drive fast, skip school, dig jazz, and get pregnant. Editors never tire of running these stories—or "surveys," as they are usually called—and the entertainment industry never tires of producing plays, records, and movies that squire us into the troubled realm of Puberty.

Last season the Broadway theater, the most urbane of our lively arts, had at least four hit shows dealing with the sensitive, awkward teen-ager who cannot communicate with his elders. They were *Look Homeward, Angel; The Dark at the Top of the Stairs; West Side Story;* and *Blue Denim.* They were all impeccably acted and directed. But by the time *Blue Denim* came along, late in the season, an adult might be excused for wishing that the play had a different theme. In this case the teen-age boy was unable to tell his parents, though they were endearingly eager to help him, that he had got a fifteen-year-old girl with child and had just sent her to a local abortionist. I found it very depressing. I can't help thinking that there are a few happy teen-agers left, and I'd like to hear about them sometime, if I have to hear about teen-agers at all —and obviously I do.

Certainly they shape the popular music of America. They buy most of the "pop" records, and the industry naturally gives them what they want. I don't object to this. They can play these discs on their own phonographs twenty-four hours a day, for all I care. But these records also dominate the public outlets, such as the jukebox and the radio. Lucky is the adult who can spin the dial and not meet the ululating minstrels of Teendom. The throbbing tunes seem to be on every station. Many of them are introduced by disc jockeys —I mean deejays—who preside over disc clubs that have millions of loyal members. The deejay talks an argot as inscrutable as burglars' cant, and he holds his listeners in thrall by bestowing on them the priceless gift of hearing their favorite record on the air. "You asked for it, Betty Ann Battenbarton of 4132-27 18th Street, Ozone Park, Queens, and so . . . *here it is!*" Miss Battenbarton's choice tune, as it turns out, could have been taped in Papua by Margaret Mead for all the sense it makes to someone of voting age.

Once in a great while the deejay plays a song that I know. This happens because disc club members are allowed to request their mothers' favorite record. At such moments I picture a silver-haired old lady and expect a fragment of Victor Herbert. Instead her favorite is a Sinatra hit of the early 1940's. (Mom is only thirty-three now.) I'm always grateful for a curio of this kind from my own youth, though I'm sure the record is a horrid waste of time to all the teen-agers who are listening, including the gal who requested it for her square old mater. Probably they flick the radio off until the song is over or use the interlude to go for a beer.

Movies are almost as teen-oriented. You know this if you have ever tried telephoning the theaters in your neighborhood some evening to find a film that uses the screen as a mature medium for mature people. When one does come along, like *The Bridge on the River Kwai*, adults go to great lengths to see it. They are hungry for good pictures. But most movies deal with the antics of immature people. They are dewy love affairs waged by the likes of Tab Hunter and Natalie Wood, switch-blade fights in the school corridors, rhythm orgies fomented by Alan Freed, and other dramas of crime and pregnancy among the young unmarrieds.

These bleak charades will not woo many grownups back into the movie house, although to judge by the moans that keep emerging from Hollywood, the industry misses them badly. In the past decade, America's weekly movie audience has shrunk from ninety million to forty-five million, and while that still leaves a lot of people, it also leaves quite a dent in the annual earnings.

Who are today's movie-goers in America? Last year Hollywood conducted a poll and found that three-quarters of them are under twenty-five years old, and half are under eighteen. Obviously Hollywood has driven away a vast segment of the adult population. Any other industry, in such a fix, would try to win its older patrons back. Instead, the movie companies seem to be saying, "If most of our customers are kids, we'll make most of our movies for kids."

Television is not dominated by the teen-ager—yet. It is a medium that comes into the home, and that's one place where teen-agers don't want to be. Their citadels are the movie house and the drive-in, their fiddlers are the jukebox, the car radio, and the dance band. But TV could capture the teens some day; it could turn up in that home-away-from-home, the back seat of the car. And if it did, the medium would be lost to the rest of America.

One portent of this dark day was the production of *Aladdin* last spring. Sparing no expense, CBS-TV hired our most sophisticated humorist, S. J. Perelman, and most debonair song writer, Cole Porter, to confect a new version of this ancient fable. It engaged the elegant Cyril Ritchard to play a wizard and the suave Basil Rathbone as emperor of China, and spent lavish sums to cloak the musical in the ornate trappings of old Cathay.

Finally, to play the boy who rubs the golden lamp, CBS signed Sal Mineo. Mineo is a nice boy, despite his somewhat delinquent mien, and he has legions of admirers in the teen-age set, as any student of fan magazines will attest. Could this possibly be the reason he was chosen for the role? It could. In fact, there could be no other reason, as millions of expectant viewers saw to their dismay when he first slouched into their range of vision, still looking like Jimmy Dean's pal in *Rebel Without a Cause*, to punish Perelman's lines. The magic disappeared, and so did a good many viewers, and so undoubtedly did a fair amount of Du Pont's money.

The real danger of teen-agism in the arts is that it builds no future, no continuity between the generations. For what will today's teen-agers do for entertainment when *they* grow up? Or is everybody forgetting that they *do* grow up? Yes, sir, every year quite a few of them turn twenty. Of course they lose their rights then as shapers of the American idiom. No editor will send a reporter near a boy who is twenty; no deejay will spin a platter for the lost souls who have gone to that country from whose bourn no teen-ager returns. Surely to reach this threshold is the blackest moment that a boy or girl can know, and I wouldn't be surprised if millions of them, now in their early twenties, are still posing as nineteen.

But the day comes when they can no longer postpone the truth, when they must be absorbed in the anonymous realm of adulthood. Then they'll see how bad things are out here. They will go to a Presley movie for lack of anything else at the local theater, and when that tousled bard first looms on the screen, the urge to squeal will have vanished like a child's runaway balloon.

William K. Zinsser, now an editorial writer for the New York Herald Tribune, *was formerly its drama editor and movie critic. He wrote* Any Old Place with You *in 1957 on his adventures in Africa and southeast Asia, and* Seen Any Good Movies Lately?, *published in December.*

ILLUSTRATIONS BY CARL ROSE

Eminent Women

On the twentieth anniversary, in 1857, of Queen Victoria's accession to the throne, an English artist named W. Warman executed this composite painting. To find 105 "Eminent Women," even including some then dead, was clearly a challenge. Most of the ladies of his choice had achieved their fame in the arts, especially literature—and a fleeting fame it has proved to be in many cases. While his choices among Victoria's subjects were highly respectable, his foreigners include such notorious females as Charlotte Corday, assassin of Marat, and the Irish actress Dorothea Jordan, who bore fifteen illegitimate children. In the key above, the Eminent Women are numbered in concentric, clockwise circles, beginning with the Queen.

1. William Shakespeare—English dramatist and poet
2. Edmund Kean—English actor
3. Nicolò Paganini—Italian violinist and composer
4. Oliver Cromwell—English statesman and military leader
5. François Arouet (Voltaire)—French writer and philosopher
6. Duc de Richelieu—French statesman and cardinal
7. Peter Paul Rubens—Flemish painter
8. John Knox—Scottish religious reformer, writer, statesman
9. Arthur Wellesley, Duke of Wellington—General and statesman
10. William Penn—English colonizer in America
11. Daniel Webster—American statesman, lawyer, orator
12. Dr. Samuel Johnson—English lexicographer, writer, critic
13. Martin Luther—Father of the Reformation in Germany
14. Lord George Gordon Byron—English poet
15. Lord Horatio Nelson—English naval leader
16. Charles Dickens—English novelist
17. Sir Henry Hardinge—English statesman and military leader
18. George Frederick Handel—German-born composer
19. Captain James Cook—English naval leader and explorer
20. Sir Walter Raleigh—English colonizer, explorer, writer
21. William Wordsworth—English poet
22. Geoffrey Chaucer—English poet
23. Nicolas Poussin—French Classical painter
24. Galileo—Italian astronomer, physicist, natural philosopher
25. Sir Rowland Hill—English postal authority
26. Napoleon Bonaparte—Emperor of the French
27. Titian—Italian painter of the Venetian school
28. Sir Astley Cooper—English surgeon
29. François Pierre Guizot—French historian and statesman
30. John Wesley—English theologian, founder of Methodism
31. James Fenimore Cooper—American novelist
32. John Wycliffe—English religious reformer and theologian
33. Robert Burns—Scottish national poet
34. Sir Henry Bulwer—English statesman
35. Sir James Clark Ross—Scottish polar explorer
36. Sir Humphry Davy—English chemist
37. Comte Georges Louis Buffon—French naturalist
38. John Flaxman—English sculptor and draftsman
39. John Locke—English philosopher
40. Joseph Addison—English essayist, poet, statesman
41. Sir Isaac Newton—English natural philosopher, mathematician
42. George Canning—English statesman
43. John Howard—English prison reformer
44. Charles James Fox, Baron Holland—English statesman and orator
45. John Bunyan—English religious writer
46. William Blake—English poet and artist
47. Robert Bruce—King and liberator of Scotland
48. Rembrandt van Rijn—Dutch painter and etcher
49. Sir Thomas More—English writer and statesman
50. George Washington—First President of the United States
51. Sir John Moore—English military leader
52. Thomas Cranmer—Archbishop of Canterbury under Henry VIII
53. James Watt—Scottish mechanical engineer and inventor
54. Miguel de Cervantes Saavedra—Spanish novelist
55. Lord George Rodney—English admiral and statesman
56. Carolus Linnaeus—Swedish botanist
57. Thomas Chalmers—Scottish religious leader and theologian
58. John Ray—English natural historian
59. Desiderius Erasmus—Dutch scholar and Renaissance humanist
60. Washington Irving—American writer
61. Sir Ralph Abercromby—English military leader
62. Sir Robert Peel—English statesman
63. Sir Christopher Wren—English architect
64. John Milton—English poet and essayist
65. George Whitefield—English evangelist
66. Albert of Saxe-Coburg-Gotha—Queen Victoria's prince consort
67. Gevartius—Dutch poet and scholar
68. Isaac Watts—English theologian and hymn writer
69. Lord Henry Brougham—Scottish jurist and political leader
70. Oliver Goldsmith—English writer
71. John Abernethy—English surgeon
72. Francis Bacon—English philosopher, statesman, writer
73. John Hunter—English anatomist and surgeon
74. Alexander Pope—English poet and essayist
75. Torquato Tasso—Italian poet
76. Theodore Hook—English humorist and novelist
77. Lord Thomas Erskine—English statesman
78. Robert Hall—English religious writer
79. Sir Joshua Reynolds—English portrait painter
80. Gioacchino Rossini—Italian composer
81. Richard Cobden—English statesman and economist
82. Sir Walter Scott—Scottish writer
83. John Churchill, Duke of Marlborough—Military, political leader
84. Sir Richard Arkwright—English inventor
85. James Sheridan Knowles—English dramatist and actor
86. Sir Francis Drake—English navigator, explorer, privateer
87. Benjamin Franklin—American philosopher, statesman, scientist
88. Ben Jonson—English dramatist and poet
89. Edmund Spenser—English poet
90. Jeremy Taylor—English religious leader and writer
91. Nicolaus Copernicus—Polish astronomer
92. Michelangelo—Italian painter, sculptor, architect
93. William Hogarth—English artist and pictorial satirist
94. Christopher Columbus—Genoese-born explorer
95. Louis Napoleon—Emperor of the French
96. Lord John Russell—English statesman
97. Daniel O'Connell—Irish national leader and statesman
98. Sir Benjamin Brodie—English surgeon
99. David Garrick—English actor
100. David Hume—Scottish philosopher and historian
101. Laurence Sterne—English novelist
102. Thomas Wolsey—English statesman and cardinal
103. William Pitt, Earl of Chatham—English statesman
104. Sir Samuel Romilly—English legal reformer
105. Sir Edwin Henry Landseer—English animal painter
106. Sir William Herschel—English astronomer
107. Edmund Burke—English statesman, writer, philosopher
108. Antonio Canova—Italian sculptor
109. John Dryden—English dramatist and poet
110. John Smeaton—English civil engineer
111. Alphonse de Lamartine—French poet, statesman, orator
112. John Walker—English actor, elocutionist, lexicographer

Eminent Men

In making this companion panel of "Eminent Men," the artist's problem was clearly one of selection. Shakespeare occupies the place of honor, immediately surrounded by an Italian violinist, the Lord Protector, a French philosopher, a French cardinal, a Flemish artist, and an English actor. Unlike the Eminent Women on the preceding pages, a high proportion of the Eminent Men are household names, and almost all are easily identified. Even such a relatively obscure figure as Rowland Hill (No. 25) deserves his fame as the founder of the English penny postal system. In the key above, as in that on page 141, the faces in this panel are numbered in concentric, clockwise circles from the central figure.